ISSUE 1, OCTOBER 2017

AUSTRALIAN FOREIGN AFFAIRS

T0363059

Contributors

Rowan Callick is China correspondent for the *Australian*.

Jo Chandler is a freelance journalist and an educator at the University of Melbourne Centre for Advancing Journalism.

James Crabtree was the *Financial Times'* bureau chief in Mumbai.

James Curran is a professor of history at the University of Sydney and non-resident fellow at the Lowy Institute for International Policy.

John Delury is associate professor of Chinese studies at Yonsei University.

Richard Denniss is the chief economist at the Australia Institute.

Allan Gyngell is an honorary professor at the ANU.

Linda Jakobson founded China Matters, a public policy initiative.

Paul Keating served as prime minister of Australia from 1991 to 1996.

Hamish McDonald is world editor for the *Saturday Paper*.

Thomas Meaney is a fellow at the Einstein Forum in Potsdam.

George Megalogenis is a journalist, political commentator and author.

Australian Foreign Affairs is published three times a year by Schwartz Publishing Pty Ltd. Publisher: Morry Schwartz. ISBN 978-1-76064-0279 ISSN 2208-5912 ALL RIGHTS RESERVED. No part of this publication may be reproduced, stored in a retrieval system, or transmitted in any form by any means electronic, mechanical, photocopying, recording or otherwise without the prior consent of the publishers. Essays, reviews and correspondence © retained by the authors. Subscriptions – 1 year print & digital auto-renew (3 issues): $49.99 within Australia incl. GST. 1 year print and digital subscription (3 issues): $59.99 within Australia incl. GST. 2 years print & digital (6 issues): $114.99 within Australia incl. GST. 1 year digital only: $29.99. Payment may be made by MasterCard, Visa or Amex, or by cheque made out to Schwartz Publishing Pty Ltd. Payment includes postage and handling. To subscribe, fill out and post the subscription card or form inside this issue, or subscribe online: www.australianforeignaffairs.com or subscribe@australianforeignaffairs.com Phone: 1800 077 514 or 61 3 9486 0288. Correspondence should be addressed to: The Editor, Australian Foreign Affairs Level 1, 221 Drummond Street Carlton VIC 3053 Australia Phone: 61 3 9486 0288 / Fax: 61 3 9486 0244 Email: enquiries@ australianforeignaffairs.com Editor: Jonathan Pearlman. Associate Editor: Chris Feik. Consulting Editor: Allan Gyngell. Deputy Editor: Kirstie Innes-Will. Management: Caitlin Yates. Marketing: Elisabeth Young and Sophie Shanahan. Publicity: Kate Nash. Design: Peter Long. Production Coordinator: Hanako Smith. Typesetting: Tristan Main. Cover image by MarcelClemens, Shutterstock. Printed in Australia by McPherson's Printing Group.

THE BIG PICTURE

P utting aside the presumption that this nation – or any nation – has an easily defined identity, it is an interesting exercise to revisit the conclusion drawn by Australia's longest-serving prime minister as he described "the thing which sticks firmly in the mind of the average Australian."

This was 1935 and Robert Menzies, then the attorney-general, was visiting London. He was speaking against the backdrop of rising despotism and fascism and he had a comforting message for his audience at Chatham House. The thing that was firmly stuck in the mind of every Australian, he explained, "is that he is entirely British."

It quickly emerged that this claim was less firm than it appeared – and, within a decade, it came unstuck. War erupted, Canberra turned from London to Washington, and the imperial bonds loosened.

The world changed, and Australia changed with it.

Eighty-two years later, there is no shortage of foreseeably seismic foreign events that could require the nation's direction and outlook to change, or be changed. Significantly – and more so than at any other time in Australia's recent history – these challenges are occurring close to home: tensions in the South China Sea, North Korean nuclear missiles, the impact of climate change, China's rise and assertiveness, risks in the financial system, the appeal of illiberal populism.

It is still unclear whether these challenges will transform the national character and turn Australia's current attempts at self-definition – a US-allied middle power with an egalitarian bias, a migrant nation edging closer to Asia – into a quaint relic of history. But it is clear that the responses will require debate, assertiveness and creativity, and an attempt to understand Australia's evolving character and its place in the region and in the world.

It is this challenge that *Australian Foreign Affairs* will attempt to meet, both in this first issue and beyond. The publication will be independent and nonpartisan and will feature leading experts and writers from Australia and around the world. It will take a broad view of foreign affairs, covering trade, economics, security, history, culture and the environment as well as politics. Its articles will explore Australia's place in the world, while testing and challenging assumptions.

This first issue addresses the nation's most significant changes and challenges – including Australia's own changing population – and considers a range of possible outcomes and responses.

The extent to which Australia has operated independently of its two great power allies, Britain and then the United States, remains a matter of debate – a debate that is increasing in importance, as Australia prepares for a region in which postwar certainties are fading.

The big picture for Australia is being shaped not just by Donald Trump, Xi Jinping and Kim Jong-un but also by the decline of the US-backed postwar liberal order. The stakes are plainly high; the consequences remain uncertain.

Against this backdrop of threat and opportunity, Australia's foreign affairs – and the ability to develop clever and informed responses – will determine not only the country's future and prosperity but the claims that can be made about the nation's character.

Jonathan Pearlman

PAUL KEATING IN CONVERSATION

'We need to determine
a foreign policy
of our own'

The following transcript is based on two interviews with Paul Keating, conducted by Professor Nick Bisley and Dr Michael Fullilove in April 2017.

Nick Bisley: What's your sense, Paul, of the extent of change in which we are living? And what do you think are going to be the big forces with which Australia, as we look out into this changing world, is going to have to grapple?

Paul Keating: At the end of the Second World War, the Americans, particularly Roosevelt, sought an end to colonialism and succeeded. No more are the British in India, no more the Dutch in Indonesia, no more the French in Indochina.

But the Cold War snap-froze that postcolonial development, and so it was not until 1989 when the Wall came down, and 1991 when the Soviet Union was dissolved, that that bipolarity between the United States and the Soviet Union was switched off; the magnets were switched off. And all of a sudden, open regionalism becomes possible and, more than that, those great societies like India, China and Indonesia begin finding their own way. What we are living with now is the maturing of that development.

The point was that the state at the top of the system, the United States, which induced this condition, the end of the Cold War, failed to have a plan for the post-event development. It didn't understand the forces it was letting loose. And, of course, they were forces for good. These great states, riven with poverty, all of a sudden becoming major economies again. China is returning to the place it occupied at the top of the international system before the Industrial Revolution. This was inconceivable in 1989 or 1990. So the world is returning to the shape it had before the Industrial Revolution.

Bisley: But what does that mean – to now go back to the world in which scale, size, population has, once again, a kind of straight line correlation to power and influence? Does that mean we go back to a world of unremitting contest and conflict between big powerful states, in which small countries, relatively speaking, are literally at the mercy of the powerful?

Keating: Well, you're right: the Industrial Revolution broke the nexus between population and GDP. Before 1800 the work of any one of us was of equal value: we clothed ourselves, we fed ourselves, we housed ourselves, and there was no shift in productivity across the globe. So the states with the largest populations had the largest GDP, and China had the largest GDP before 1800. But all of a sudden a little state like Britain discovers congealed energy, coal, produces steam, an Industrial Revolution begins and, all of a sudden, its GDP is larger than China's.

What is happening now is that globalisation has made the availability of capital and the technology ubiquitous. We're now rejoining the link between population and GDP. We're going back to the world that obtained before the Industrial Revolution. And we're going to have these big states: India, China as well as the Atlantic states – and, yet to come, the great states of Africa. This is the world we're going to be living in.

So the days of comfortable multilateralism superintended by the United States, along sort of Jeffersonian principles, is fading to a world of great power entities and great power politics again. And that's just a much harder world for a country like Australia to live in.

Bisley: There is a sense that possibly the mood around globalisation has soured – that there's a kind of resurgent nationalism and a sense of mercantilism. What's your sense of that balance between the openness of globalisation and the nationalism that's out there?

Keating: Well, there's a difference between globalisation and globalism. What we're seeing now is a rejection of globalism, not globalisation. And globalism is not a long-dated concept. It really started after the end of the Cold War, about 1992, and finished in 2008 with the American financial crisis. So it went for less than twenty years, around twenty years. This is what the Americans talked about in the great celebration at the end of the Cold War, and in the rise of the American stock markets in the dotcom boom.

They spoke of the end of history. "It's all over," said Francis Fukuyama. It's all over, the Jeffersonians have won, the market system has won, we're going to have a world which reflects this sort of democracy, we're going to have a consensus about the way economies work, we're going to have a consensus about the world power order, with the US at the top. And so it went. And, of course, this began collapsing after Iraq and accelerated after the financial crisis in 2008.

So if you take Xi Jinping, the Chinese president, he made a speech recently in favour of globalisation. But he's absolutely opposed to globalism – the notion of lining up in a proprietary structure behind the United States in an Atlantic-dominated world with Atlantic institutions. So China is no longer interested in the IMF [International Monetary Fund] and the World Bank. They're setting up their own institutions: the AIIB [Asian Infrastructure Investment Bank], the Silk Road Fund. The Chinese financial reserves abroad are larger than the IMF's free reserves – so it has no need of the IMF.

So whenever you hear Xi Jinping speak, he always refers to a new system of global governance, which is code for saying not an American one. What the Chinese want is a UN-based one. And so, therefore, this is not a rejection of globalisation – that is, the ubiquity of the money and the technology – it's not a rejection of that or the trade that comes with it. It's a rejection of the "one size fits all" strategic policy.

Bisley: You've spoken several times about the need for China to be given space and for China to be accommodated. What do you think the region looks like? How comfortable are we, as a liberal-democratic society, with a China-centric Asia, with the Chinese Communist Party at the centre of it?

Keating: Well, whether we are comfortable or not, it's with us. What is happening in China knows no precedent in world economic history. There has been nothing like this before and nothing will ever be like it again. Because we won't ever have one and a quarter billion people so competently directed by a single authority, as we have now. I mean, even if India, at roughly the same population, kicks on, the chances of them doing what the Chinese have done is low. Or even a bunch of African states. China and its development is wealth on a scale we have never seen before.

So the idea that this great economy is going to be a strategic client of the United States – that they will be kept in line by US naval patrols – is, of course, nonsense. But this is what Hillary Clinton and Barack Obama's pivot was all about. It was about the embedment of US power, and with it the maintenance of US hegemony in Asia.

It's simply unreal, and we should not remain party to this piece of flummery. That's not to say we don't need the US strategically in Asia as a balancing and conciliating power. We do. But if we are party to the nonsense that we should line up with the United States to maintain its strategic hegemony in Asia over China, we must have troubles – great, great troubles. So I'm hoping that this new relationship between Trump and Xi Jinping is one where the US starts to wake up to the recognition about scale and power: that military power comes with and is a reflection of economic power.

Before the Industrial Revolution, China was on the top of the system and had a tributary system of states which bowed and genuflected to them. Let's hope we're not going to be bowing and genuflecting. But the reality is that the power is there, and we would be well advised to begin assimilating it – adjusting ourselves to it – instead of trying to hide behind an American "guarantee" like a bunch of loyal little Americans. "What we need is more Uncle Sam." You know the tune.

Bisley: How does a country like Australia influence a country like China, given the disparity of scale?

Keating: By being a bit clever. I talked the Chinese into the whole notion of a Pacific leaders' meeting with APEC. Kevin Rudd encouraged them into the East Asia Summit. We were doing clever things, but if you insist upon being dumb you will be treated accordingly.

Bisley: We've had this international period where our values are being neatly aligned and defended by a global order that's broadly in line with those. We're now entering a world in which our values are going to be just one of a series of values that are in competition, if you like. How do we advocate for and defend those values?

Keating: We do believe in those values but we should be careful what we attempt to propagate. The Americans are insisting they are the exceptional country with these values, that it is their mission to propagate those values. And we've seen that propagation in Iraq, we've seen the propagation in the Arab Spring, we've seen the same propagation in Libya.

And so the idea that the Chinese state, with its Communist Party, which brought it together, and its general Confucian sense of self, should, in some way, accommodate a set of broadly East Coast American values, shared by the likes of ourselves, is simply a naive view of how China ought to be managed.

That's not to say that we condone abuses of human rights in China. We don't and we've spoken about them often. But in the end, China is a patchwork quilt of prosperities. To achieve what they have, taking 600 million people from poverty, requires a large measure of central government authority. No OECD country could ever have done what the Chinese have done. Not one.

So what human value do we attach to lifting someone out of abject poverty; of taking 600 million of them out of poverty to live good lives in decent accommodation, with proper clothing, medicines, etc.? Or are we just hung up about the fact that some detainees don't get proper legal representation – you know? Where, in our mind, is the weight of equity in judgements about the Chinese, what they've actually produced, what they've actually done? So human values go to more than simply human rights of the kind we normally associate ourselves with and make judgements about.

Bisley: That's sort of collective advancement of the Chinese people weighed against the rights of individuals, and clearly we know where the Party falls down on that one.

Keating: Nation-building is a tough caper. The Communist Party pulled the country together after European imperialism and the Japanese had ripped it apart, and that government of theirs has been the most competent government in the world in the last thirty years.

Bisley: So do you think – or to what extent do you think – President Trump presents a risk to Asia or to Australia in its policies and its outlook?

Keating: Well, as American presidents go, he's obviously the wild joker in the pack. We don't know really how he will conduct himself.

But he's had a couple of reasonable ideas: one is that the US should have a better relationship with China, and we'd all applaud that, because the sort of lives we live in this country depend upon the US and China finding common cause in the Pacific. So if there's peace in the Pacific, our lives are going to be that much better.

And the other idea he had was to have a better relationship with Russia. That great state that has essentially borne the brunt of West European militarism, with Bonaparte, with Hitler and now in a sort of stand-off with the EU. And so the great challenge for the Americans is to find a place for Russia in the European construct. Not that Russia will ever be part of the EU system, but to find some point of harmony and accommodation. The Americans decided not to do this by extending NATO in 1997; by biting off bits of the old Soviet bloc, Hungary, Poland, the Czech Republic and later the Baltic states – all into NATO. And, of course, this produced, among Russian nationalists, a great reaction. In a sense, the Americans created Putin.

So Trump may be the wildcard, but maybe we will make progress on these two big fronts.

Michael Fullilove: You were, much earlier than anyone else I know, talking about Trump as a possible victor. What was it that you saw in Trump himself?

Keating: Well, the enormous inner confidence. He's a momentum player, basically. Probably a narcissist. There's a bit of that in all of us. Hillary Clinton's problem was she didn't have a story and Trump had a story.

The displacement of people in factories in America happened thirty years ago. Billy Joel wrote that song, "Allentown," how "we're living here in Allentown, and they're closing all the factories down. Out in Bethlehem they're filling out forms and standing in line" in 1983. It was on then. And Trump's saying he's got the remedy now. Of course, there is no remedy. His policy is a con, fundamentally; it's not going to work.

And the people of Ohio will wake up at some point to that fact. But the point is Trump as president might just induce a shift in growth and wealth of a kind they get some part of, and if he can kick that economy of his along by half a per cent or 1 per cent of GDP, he'll get a second term.

Fullilove: Australia – the culture of Australia – is changing fundamentally. To what extent do you see that as beginning to play into how Australia thinks about itself and the world, and the way it identifies with its foreign policy and shapes its foreign policy orientation?

Keating: All of the states we have mentioned tonight – Russia, the United States, China – they all have countries on their borders. We don't. So we've been given a great inheritance. I mean, right now, if you had any footwork, you would be in there trying to reorder the whole East Asian system to suit us. That's what I was trying to do back twenty-five years ago with the APEC leaders' meeting – getting the US engaged in Asia; getting China into the compact; sitting the Chinese and the Japanese down together; us sitting down with the Indonesians.

You would take these issues on today with such gusto. But you've got to do some things right. You've got to say, we can't have the monarch of another country as our head of state; we can't have a flag with the flag of another country in its corner; we can't maintain the policy that we have in respect of the indigenes. Notwithstanding a lot of interest and kindliness on the part of the Australian community, we've never actually busted that problem. So we should be going to Asia as a new Australian nation, as a continent which has turned a new leaf.

Fullilove: What role does the [US] alliance play, or should the alliance play, for an Australia that's carrying out a more distinctive role for itself in a world in which China plays a much greater role in our future?

Keating: If you've been in a strategic partnership of the kind we have had with the United States for 100 years, do you have to fear every week that they may not like what you say about this or that matter, or that you may not join them in escapades in some country or another? Really? I mean, you'd have to have a low sense of self-regard and a low sense of confidence to think that somehow you would lose the support of the Americans. We would never lose the Americans.

Who else around this part of the world has a continent, an English language culture, a common jurisprudence? We couldn't shake the

Americans off even if we tried. That is the truth. But no, the policy flakes here think that we had better send a boat through the South China Sea because some American admiral in Honolulu has suggested if we don't, the Americans are going to think badly of us. This is all defeatist and bad-think.

The truth is the Americans are entirely important to the peace and good order of East Asia. And having them there as a balancing power, as Britain was in Europe in the nineteenth century, is a good thing. When Bonaparte was afoot, and later with the Germans conquering the rest of Europe, Britain stood off as the balancing power. It did it with Kaiser Wilhelm in the 1900s, as it did in the run-up to the First World War. It had that balancing and conciliating role.

Similarly, I think the Americans should enjoy that role in Asia; and more than that, we need them to. That's the point: we need them to. But what we don't need them doing, or trying to do, is to maintain the game as it was at the end of the Second World War, or attempting to turn China into a client state. The Chinese will never be a strategic client state of the United States. That policy will not work.

So what will work? Being a balancer and a conciliator. But if you say that today to the policy wimp brigade here in Australia, they say, "This is an affront to the United States."

The fact is, we can do better and we can articulate a place for the Americans that they, at this point, are incapable of articulating for themselves.

Fullilove: The central theme of Allan [Gyngell]'s book [*Fear of Abandonment: Australia in the World since 1942*] is that a principal driver of Australian foreign policy is our fear of being abandoned by great and powerful friends. How important is that as a theme, and what are the other big themes in Australian foreign policy?

Keating: Well, I think that's been the primary theme. Allan is right in identifying it and the title of the book says it all. As he says in the book, this all began with imperial adventurism in the first place – what he calls the audacious claim to a continent. Here we arrive, 400 yards away from here, in a couple of little wooden boats and we claim the whole Australian continent. Audacious is an understatement.

And, being a lot of good little Britons, we continued with the whole idea of the British Empire until, of course, Britain let us down in Singapore in 1942. So we were dragged to Asia by the Second World War, then found another guarantor: the United States. Some of us learnt that lesson and some of us didn't. I've always believed we had to find our security in Asia and not from Asia.

Even the mere fact we were looking for a strategic guarantor meant we did not have a closed mind; we were out there, at least on the highways and byways. And Allan records in the book the things which we've done in the postwar years: the Chemical Weapons Convention; the Cambodia peace accords; the APEC structure, including the leaders' meetings; the G20, Kevin [Rudd]'s involvement with that and the East Asia Summit.

I think it's getting harder for us to do those things, but the underlying impetus that fed it all was fear of abandonment. And, of course, this quasi-religious, now sacramental, view we have of the American alliance is fed by that fear.

Fullilove: You're a little different from some Labor foreign policymakers who are more focused, perhaps, on institutions and questions of human rights. So what was the big picture for you on foreign policy when you served as prime minister?

Keating: Well, I had a great advantage, of course: I wasn't a lawyer. That meant I began with a wider field of view. And legalism has informed these institutional issues far too much and for far too long in Australia.

We saw these shifts of power from Britain to Europe and then from Europe to the United States in the last gasp of the nineteenth century and the turn of the twentieth century. And we've now seen that happen again with the shift in economic power from the West to the East, and – in broad economic terms, at least – a sharing of economic power between the United States and China. When these things happen, the strategic settings change.

There's another thing. You pick up ideas in public life. One of the ideas I've picked up was that great states need strategic space, and if you don't give it to them they'll take it. This has been true of all of them – Britain, the United States, Germany, Japan – and you can see it now, to some extent, with China. So I think these things drive policy. Also, simply having a clear idea about motive, people's motives, looking behind the screen and seeing what people really mean, what their aspirations are really about, is central to judgements.

Fullilove: When you were serving as prime minister, were there prime ministers that you'd look back on in terms of the way they managed Australian foreign policy and think that there was something very impressive that that PM did?

Keating: There's nothing that has ever been really impressive about Australian foreign policy – that's the truth of it. The best we've ever done was, of course, Curtin and his arrangement with the Americans in the prosecution of the Pacific War. But look at Menzies and Suez, you know; look at him again in Vietnam. I mean, these are not policies you'd yodel about, are they?

The break, you would say, was Whitlam's recognition of China and his determination to have a relationship with Asia. Allan makes a point: this all starts with the Statute of Westminster, which was what, 1942? So before that you had [Richard] Casey saying the foreign policy of Great Britain was in essence the foreign policy of Australia. That's where we were.

There is much now made by the Liberals about the American alliance – but that was like putting your foot into an old shoe by that stage.

Of course, in those days there weren't many European-type societies with a big continent like us, so there was no way the Americans were going to let us go. I mean, the so-called alliance agreement wouldn't have taken too much effort to sort out.

So you say, well, what are the big things in Australian foreign policy since? Well, I think scrambling off the ground, getting the APEC structure together, getting the East Asia Summit together, Kevin [Rudd]'s involvement with the G20 are the first bloom, if you like, of Australian foreign policy, but in a much more independent frame of mind. More self-reliant and self-starting, not sitting back waiting for a friend, as we're still doing, to tell us what to do.

Fullilove: You got a lot of attention at the end of last year when you said that Australia should "cut the tag" with the United States. But, of course, you have a long history of defending the alliance in other forums, in the forum of the Labor Party over many decades, and one of your motivations in trying to stand up the APEC leaders' meeting was to ensure the United States remained engaged with the region. So what did you mean when you said Australia should "cut the tag" with the United States, and how important do you think the alliance is to Australia's national interests?

Keating: Well, "to cut the tag" was a flow of thoughts and a phrase. I said we have tag-along rights and we should cut the tag – meaning, we should have rights independent of tag-along rights. I didn't mean cut the alliance. Even if we had no document anymore, we would remain friends with the United States into the future.

We've been in every battle, as everyone knows, since the First World War. We share a lot of cultural and historical common ground.

But this idea that we have to be the Uriah Heeps of this world, dragging along behind them... whereas we should be running an altogether independent foreign policy with much more independence within this alliance structure. The idea that we need signals from Washington to find direction... I mean, this is a state which has done fantastic things for the world but has also made mistakes – large mistakes.

So, therefore, Australia should be putting its interests first and within the context of an alliance which is never going to fade away. The point is the United States is entirely important to the governance of East Asia. It's important they remain in this part of the world and a force. I've always thought that. Always said that.

The Americans had a chance at the end of the Cold War of reshaping the world but they completely failed the opportunity. I said this to Bill Clinton at the time: the United States should have framed and guaranteed; they should have been the framer and guarantor of the Atlantic. They had the pond itself, the Atlantic, they had NATO and they had the European Union. The one task for them in consolidating Europe was to bring Russia into the Europe construct and they would have consolidated their power there.

But they can never be the framer and the guarantor in Asia. Not now. In 1945, certainly – but not now. In Asia, they should be the balancer and the conciliator, because the idea that China is going to be a strategic client of the United States is nonsense. China is returning to where it was before the Industrial Revolution; it's returning to being the primary economic state of the world, and it's now a long way into that task.

And what they are doing in the South China Sea, they're marking out the space like a tiger does, you know. The tiger rubs itself against the trees to let any other tiger know, "This is my space." And, of course, the Americans had taken the same view about Cuba and the Caribbean. And, as we know, any American cruiser could take out each of those emplacements on these islets the Chinese have created in an instant, so strategically these islets don't add up to much.

But the point is the Chinese are attempting to superintend the corner of one ocean while the Americans are trying to superintend three oceans: the Atlantic, the Mediterranean and the Pacific. It can't be done. It is strategic overstretch and it is unlikely to be a successful strategy. So the "pivot," which I criticised on the night it was announced, was bound to fail. But nor do we want China to be the dominant state in East Asia in a strategic sense. This is why we need the United States here, as the floating good guys, letting people know there are balances.

I always remind American admirals that every great battleship went down in its first week at sea in the Second World War: the *Bismarck*, the *Tirpitz* and the *Yamato*. Churchill sent the *Renown* and the *Repulse* to Malaysia. It wasn't their first week at sea but their first conflict, and they went down too. Just as these American carriers are going to go down when the fight turns nasty.

And I said to this admiral, "They all sound the same, you know, in the end." He said, "What do you mean?" I said, "Glug, glug, glug, glug."

Following Charlemagne's return after the Huns and the Visigoths, the shape of Europe broadly aped the earlier Roman Empire. And there was a natural balance of states within it. But Asia has never been like that – it has always been a hierarchy with China at the top. So, in this part of the world, what constitutes balance, what constitutes a Westphalian-type system of balance in East Asia is hard to know, but it should include the United States.

I hold the view that Asia will never be reshaped by a non-Asian power, and certainly not by the application of an American military force. If we accept that point, we need to keep the Americans as the floating good guys, to secure them in the balancing role. But as far as we are concerned, we need to determine a foreign policy of our own – one that looks after Australia's interest in the new order; an order which will have China as its centre of gravity.

Fullilove: What about all of China's neighbours? Do they have to accept China's prerogatives, for example, in the South China Sea?

Keating: Well, they probably won't, but they will probably do a trade with the Chinese, come to some settlement. But we shouldn't go steaming naval vessels through the South China Sea in a fight that's not ours.

So telling the Americans this is not our fight, we're not in it, is something we should do. Look at the Philippines president and his attitude.

But, of course, the problem is – and this is particularly true of the current government – it has an attitude to the United States and our relationship with it which is not in any way at odds with that which was obtained during the Cold War. For them, nothing has changed. It is as if China hasn't happened. There is a great state rising in the East, with all its magnetic power, both strategic and economic, but to the Julie Bishops of the world – they will put all their bets on black. This is the nonsense John Howard used to go on with: we don't have to choose between China and the United States. Well, we're choosing every day; the choices are on all the time.

Fullilove: How do you think President Trump's foreign policy is shaping up?

Keating: Well, I've taken some heart from the fact he seems to have developed a reasonable relationship with Xi Jinping at the meeting they had in Florida, and also the fact that the Chinese have put their hand up to do something about North Korea.

You see, I think the strategic competition between the United States and China in the Pacific in a broad sense is almost resolved. No important or sensible American thinks that China is going to become a strategic client of the United States as envisaged in the Nixon–Mao deal. The Nixon–Mao deal was arrived at to deal with Soviet divisions on China's borders. When the Soviet Union was dissolved in 1991, the underpinnings of the deal fell away, except the Chinese were not then powerful enough to push the Americans away, but they are powerful enough now. The fact is China will not and will never become a strategic client of the United States in the way Japan has over the last seventy years.

And you can see American impotence in the fact that notwithstanding the pivot which President Obama announced in our parliament and the fact that the Chinese have now built these islets in the South China Sea, they gave the Americans a test. They said, "We're going to build these islets," and the Americans fundamentally failed to respond. Obama made a hairy-chested speech about it in Tokyo and nothing else happened.

No document will ever set out the prerogatives and the powers of the United States and China in the Pacific. It will never be written. State understandings will only come from testing, pressure and counter-pressure. The Chinese have done their testing; they believe they had Obama's measure. The islets are now a fact of life. I believe China's real ambitions are in the west, down the Silk Road, and not in the east.

So the great challenge for Europe and the United States is in consolidation of the Atlantic, given that they are unable to consolidate Asia. There has to be a settlement of some kind between Russia and Europe. Maybe a guy like Trump can manage it because no one else ever wanted to do it, not Clinton, not George W. [Bush], not Obama. So I give him marks for that. So what you've got to do now is to work out what you can do with him. But one thing not to do with the Americans is keep bowing. This is just bad behaviour, very bad behaviour – counterproductive behaviour.

Audience member: Mr Keating, when you were prime minister you were associated with the attack on the cultural cringe ... Are we culturally equipped to avoid falling into the trap of a strategic cringe towards China?

Paul Keating: Well, I should certainly hope so. Allan recorded me saying in the book – and I used to say this to the cabinet – when they were giving out continents, not many people got one, but we did. We have a border with no one. So we don't have the kind of disputes that most states have. Look at the number of countries on China's border. Same for the United States. We don't have these issues.

It therefore gives us enormous flexibility, and there is also a rising centre of economic gravity in South-East Asia, particularly in Indonesia. So we can make our way in this part of the world. I've been saying for years South-East Asia and the ASEAN group of states is where we should be devoting much more time and attention.

But, that said, the economic rise of China is without precedent in human history. We've never seen anything like it and never will, and we haven't seen it in full bloom yet. When we went to school, the teachers would often put iron filings on a piece of paper and put a magnet underneath and very quickly all the iron filings would line up in the magnetic field of the magnet. That will happen in this part of the world.

But China is a lonely state, a big state but a lonely one, and it is always looking for friends. Therefore, if we go back to the business of creating APECs and East Asia Summits and we start thinking again, in somewhere like ASEAN, for instance, we could do a lot. We could make that whole thing work much better. ASEAN would be happy we were making it work better and the United States would be happy if it was working better.

In other words, self-reliance and self-help should be the keynote of our foreign policy. We don't want to become a tributary of China reminiscent of the old tributary system they had in the seventeenth and eighteenth centuries. We have to resist that. And we can't afford China to become the sole and predominant economic power. That's why it's so important the United States remains involved in the Western Pacific, so important. So a clever state does this dance. It's only a dumb state which gets caught up in some signalling system of the kind we seem to have always found ourselves in. ∎

The interview with Nick Bisley, Professor of International Relations at La Trobe University, was conducted at the Melbourne Recital Centre in Melbourne, and the interview with Dr Fullilove, the Executive Director of the Lowy Institute, at the Lowy Institute in Sydney. The transcripts have been approved with slight revisions by Mr Keating.

THE COMPANY WE KEEP

Risk and reward
in the time
of Trump

Allan Gyngell

Australian foreign policy has never had to deal with a world like this. For sixty years the international system seemed to be moving towards a world that was ever more integrated. The path was never smooth, but whatever its twists and pitfalls, the destination seemed clear. Driven by the ambition and power of the United States, the overwhelming victor of World War II, a new international system was created in which multilateral institutions like the United Nations and the World Bank would help secure peace and prosperity. New states in Asia and Africa threw off their colonial bonds and joined the global community. Later in the twentieth century, the technologies of the information revolution made possible the investment flows and supply chains of economic globalisation, helping to bring some of the largest of those states into the global economy.

But by the close of the first decade of the twenty-first century, the journey's end seemed more uncertain. Terrorist attacks in New York and Washington in September 2001, followed by the two great policy catastrophes of the early millennium – the invasion of Iraq and the global financial crisis – disrupted the politics of Western societies. The technological innovations that had promised to bind the world together as a global village had instead generated economic upheaval and sharpened divisions, allowing new allegiances to be built across national boundaries and introducing a complex cyber domain into global strategic competition. Small Salafi-jihadist groups fortified by a theology of martyrdom showed that terrorists could – with little or no weaponry or training – threaten the security of citizens and massively shift the allocation of a state's resources. Millions of refugees and displaced people trying to escape the turmoil in the Middle East and North Africa strained the sense of solidarity in Western countries.

The weight of global power shifted slowly, but with increasing speed, eastwards, taking with it chunks of the established manufacturing jobs of the developed world. China's economy, less than half that of the United States in 2004, became the largest in the world by some measurements. As China's economy grew, so did its defence budget, making it capable of contesting the United States' military primacy, which had shaped East Asia since World War II.

Meanwhile, in Europe and North America, the jobs of workers from truckers to lawyers were threatened by new technologies like robotics, artificial intelligence and 3D printing.

Policymakers stabbed away at familiar buttons but the responses were sluggish. Assurances that open trade and investment would deliver growth and that democratic systems would ensure the fruits of that growth were equitably distributed sounded increasingly hollow to Western voters. Wages were falling, inequality rising and productivity stagnating.

The foreign and economic policy elites who had delivered these conditions seemed to be the last people you would want to lead you out. The 2017 Edelman Trust Barometer, which surveyed citizens in seventeen countries, showed a precipitate drop in their trust in media, government and business; 53 per cent of respondents believed the current system had failed them. The policymakers and pundits of Washington, London and Canberra appeared increasingly like the Hollywood executives so famously characterised by the screenwriter William Goldman: "Nobody knows anything."

In the resulting uncertainty, cosmopolitan hopes and globalising norms were elbowed aside by nationalist political goals, protectionist economic aims and nativist cultural instincts. In his inaugural address in 1961, President John F. Kennedy spoke to and about "citizens of the world." President Trump's senior national security and economic advisers, H.R. McMaster and Gary Cohn, declared, in contrast, that "the world is not a 'global community' but an arena where nations, non-governmental actors and businesses engage and compete for advantage." This was not just a Western phenomenon: by 2017 strongly nationalist leaders had taken power in Russia, China, Japan, India and Turkey.

The question for Australia is how it can remain prosperous and secure in a world whose current form and future trajectory seem so uncertain. What can it change, and where must it adjust? How can Australia maximise the options available to it? Foreign policy will be central to its response.

A nation's success depends on many things – a strong economy, a cohesive society, robust institutions, an effective defence force. All these elements comprise statecraft, and foreign policy is the dimension of statecraft that engages most directly with the outside world. Its purpose is to expand the space in the international system within which the state can operate, making sure that in the constant flux of world politics its interests are protected and that choices are always available to policy-makers so the country is not forced or coerced along particular paths.

The end of the postwar order

A country like Australia, which has global interests but not enough clout to get what it wants by throwing its weight around, will always be better off in a world where negotiated rules – which it has played a part in setting – prevail over ad hoc deals. That applies to everything from the environment to the rules of war. It's the reason successive Australian governments have worked hard to help build the structures like the United Nations and the World Trade Organization where the rules are made.

All Australian governments have declared their support for a rules-based international order, but what does that mean? Phrases such as "rules-based order," "liberal international order" and "existing order" are often used interchangeably. Foreign Minister Julie Bishop told a Singapore audience in March 2017 that "the long and prosperous peace" depended on the continuation of "the liberal rules-based order." Malcolm Turnbull has said the maintenance of regional dynamism depends on the "rules-based structure that has enabled it." But these are different things. A rules-based order is simply one in which the rules are agreed by the states involved. It doesn't much matter what those rules are. All it requires is negotiation and reciprocal commitment. The International Civil Aviation Organization doesn't require a particular set of values to be embedded in its regulations to prevent planes from crashing into each other. In contrast, the liberal international order was the specific system which emerged from the US-led efforts to remake the world at the end of World War II. Its characteristics included an open international trading system; new institutions, such as the United Nations, with universal membership, a security system anchored by a network of American security alliances; and the promotion of liberal norms in areas like human rights. Its liberal aims (contrasting with the earlier state-centred Westphalian system) were backed by American power.

But that postwar order, in the way we have known it, is over – for several reasons. New states want greater say in the way the rules are set. No consensus exists on what those rules should be. And in areas such as open trade, the US administration has backed away from some of its founding principles. As a result, global rule-making is at a low ebb and the institutions that support it are increasingly weak and frayed. It is unclear what will come next, but the status quo certainly can't be sustained.

Values and national identity

The coinage of foreign policy is national interests. These are usually clear and measurable. You can readily trade away an investment approval limit for a higher beef quota. But no Australian government can sustain a foreign policy based entirely on hard-nosed "reasons of state." Voters want their country's behaviour to reflect something of themselves in the world.

Beyond core beliefs in representative democracy, the rule of law and freedom of expression, individual Australians place different weights on the values they hold. This is reflected in the foreign policy debate. "How can Australia engage deeply with a China ruled by a repressive authoritarian government?" ask some. "How can Australia ask China to abide by international rules in the South China Sea while ignoring its own obligations under the United Nations Refugees Convention?" demand others.

Fitting values into foreign policy is hard. How do you balance your interests and values? Where do you intervene and where do you stand aside? In foreign policy, values are almost always easiest to support in circumstances where national interests are less intense. But apart from Australia and New Zealand, all the countries in East and South Asia, including Japan and India, rank somewhere between flawed democracies and authoritarian regimes in the Economic Intelligence Unit's 2017 democracy index. Where in this messy continuum does Australia seek to apply pressure, and where do we keep quiet? The judgements are seldom clear-cut.

The content of our foreign policy and the way it is implemented are intimately connected with our national identity. This has changed greatly over the years. At various times, Australians have seen themselves as builders of the British Empire, representatives of a beleaguered white race in a sea of Asians, a pillar of the West in a global cold war, a loyal American ally, a successful multicultural society seeking its future in Asia, or a model international citizen. Aspects of all these images, separately and together, have formed the basis of a long national debate. This debate will now be conducted by a very different Australian society. A new generation of policymakers, whose experiences and memories don't go back much before the turn of the century and who have never known an unconnected world, will soon be in charge. And the Australian community now includes more than two and a half million people who were born in Asia. Both the millennials and the migrants will understand the past – and therefore imagine the future – in new ways. They will be less inclined to see geography as predicament, and less given to thinking about themselves as regional outsiders. These demographic shifts will challenge and change Australia just as deeply as did, in the 1960s and '70s, the slow drift away from our sense of being part of a broader British family. The debate about the symbols of our national sovereignty, such as our head of state, will take on new importance as this very different Australian community moves to preserve a cohesive social identity in a more incoherent and atomised world.

This world presents specific challenges in the places that matter most to Australia, and demands careful and calculated changes in the way it approaches all its key relationships. The leadership of the United States and the growing weight of China lie at the centre of the foreign policy debate for Australia.

The United States

From the months after the first British fleet arrived in Port Jackson, anxiety about how the new settlers could sustain their audacious claim to a great continent generated a deep fear of abandonment, which has left its mark on Australian foreign policy ever since. The first and most deeply rooted of the responses we had to that fear was the search for an alliance with a great and powerful friend. First we looked to Britain for our security, then, after World War II, to the United States.

In 2017, Lowy Institute polling confirmed that around three-quarters of Australians, whatever their views on specific American policies, believe that the alliance is very or fairly important to Australia's security. That figure has been remarkably consistent throughout the thirteen years of Lowy polling. But in 2016 American voters elected as president a man who disdained many of the foundational beliefs of the postwar global order the United States had put in place. He criticised the open international trading system, cast doubt on the value of alliances and stepped back from global agreements. Even his allegiance to some of the core values of democracy and the rule of law seemed slippery and casual. His views aligned with the instincts of many of his supporters, who felt themselves marginalised by globalisation and threatened by outsiders. For them, "America First" was a compelling message.

The United States is a resilient country with a flexible economy, a free society and some of the world's best research institutions. It will remain more important globally than any other state. But America is changing. Its politics are deeply divided and its institutions of government struggling to deliver. Its relative power in the world is declining. That truth is neither surprising nor unwelcome – it reflects the fact that global development is working. But it requires Americans to adjust to a less tractable world.

Although democracy will almost certainly deliver a future president better suited to the job than Donald Trump, it is by no means clear that Trump's view of America's role in the world is an aberration. More likely, historians will come to see in Barack Obama and Donald Trump merely different political responses to the same changing international order: evidence of a United States no longer willing or able to bear any burden or pay any price to maintain its global leadership.

That has consequences for Australia. In the twenty-first century, the Australia–United States relationship has been decked out in a military uniform. Wars in the Middle East, deeper intelligence links forged in the global war on terror and new defence capabilities encouraged closer military integration at all levels. Like the Almighty, the Alliance acquired a capital letter in official documents. But as Australia adjusts to a post-hegemonic United States, it needs to think more deeply about what the US–Australia relationship means, and what the ANZUS Treaty involves. As Paul Keating points out, it is inconceivable, even without a mutual defence treaty, that Australia and the United States would not have a deep relationship of central importance to both of us. It could hardly be otherwise for two English-speaking nations, migrant societies intimately connected at the personal level and benefiting from strong trade and economic links.

That is not an argument for abandoning the alliance – all other considerations apart, this is no time for Australia to be ditching a central instrument of its international engagement – but Australia needs to be clearer about what the obligations of the alliance are, and where its interests coincide with or diverge from Washington's, to strip away the sentimentality that can entrap us and impede our American friends from seeing us clearly. By helping to force that necessary review, Donald Trump may turn out to be an unexpected friend of the Australia–US relationship.

China

Australia needs to put equal thought into its relationship with China. In one way or another, China will be central to all Australia's economic, strategic and political objectives. It is hard to think of an international issue – from the security of the South China Sea to development policy in Africa – where China's decisions will not be important. Inside Australia, the impact of growing Chinese investment, the presence of rising numbers of Chinese students and tourists, and the role of Chinese Australians in politics and public debate will become increasingly significant.

The most powerful Chinese leader since Deng Xiaoping, President Xi Jinping is drawing on nationalism and economic growth to legitimise the Communist Party's control. He is asserting a more central position for China, partly by moving into spaces vacated by the US administration: defending globalisation, standing by the Paris Agreement on climate change and embarking on massive new infrastructure developments throughout Eurasia with his "Belt and Road Initiative."

Before today's Australian primary school students leave high school it is likely that China will be the world's largest economy by any measure. That is not to underestimate the difficulties ahead. China's leaders face huge problems, including growing debt, social inequality and environmental degradation. It is still unclear whether an authoritarian political system can generate the creativity and innovation necessary to sustain growth and social harmony. But it would be a dangerous mistake for any Australian policymaker to bank on a coming China collapse, and the consequences of a failing China would be harder by far for Australia to deal with than the problems of a rising state.

All Australian governments this century have adopted a two-pronged response to China's rise, acknowledging that China will play a larger strategic role in Asia, while calling on it to do so in a way that maintains stability and the right of all the regional states to have their voices heard. As Malcolm Turnbull put it in June 2017, "China will play a larger role in shaping the region. It is natural that Beijing will seek strategic influence to match its economic weight. But we want to see China fill the leadership role it desires in a way which strengthens the regional order that has served us all so well."

It's not independence that Australian foreign policy needs, but substance, subtlety and creativity

He also repeated the comfortable and familiar line of all his recent predecessors: that a choice between Beijing and Washington "is an utterly false choice." But that is true only in the sense that Australia is unlikely ever to be confronted with an ultimatum asking it to choose between preserving its trade with China and formally abrogating the ANZUS Treaty (or to agree to do so if it were). In the real world, however, Australia is choosing every day – to join the Asia Infrastructure Investment Bank, to conduct freedom of navigation patrols in the South China Sea, to urge one course of action or another on our South-East Asian neighbours.

If it is to make the right choices, Australia's objective must be to understand the Chinese party-state political system and its leaders at least as well as it understands those of the United States. As in any large government, China's various departments, agencies and individuals have different approaches and interests. It is vital that Australia knows what these are and how the dynamics of Chinese policymaking work – not because we will always agree with China, but because we have a much better chance of shaping its behaviour if we are engaged and knowledgeable than if we are not.

This will require greater investment of human and other capital – and more time from our leaders – than anything we have tried so far. New points of contact are required across all the areas of our engagement, including policy development, research, cultural and educational links.

Japan, India and Korea

With rising Chinese power and the continuing challenge of North Korea's nuclear ambitions, Australia's relationships with the other large regional powers of North and West Asia will become even more important. The relationships with Japan and South Korea are long-standing, deep and bipartisan, underpinned by strong public support. High levels of trust have developed over decades, bilaterally and in regional institutions like APEC and the East Asia Summit.

India and Australia have taken longer to come to terms with each other. The obvious economic complementarity that exists with North Asia is absent. India has taken a different path to development and its messy and slow-moving democracy makes change difficult. But for the first time in our modern history, practical alignments of economic and political interests are becoming clearer.

It would be naive to claim that Australian efforts to engage more deeply with Japan, India and Korea do not have an element of balancing China. It would be an even greater mistake, however, to see the clear prospects for closer cooperation with these countries as no more than a hedging strategy. Substantial Australian economic, political and security interests exist here quite independently of China.

South-East Asia

Closer to home, the South-East Asian states of ASEAN are becoming a forum for strategic competition between China and the United States. There are worrying precedents here. In earlier periods of great power competition in the region, East–West competition in the Cold War produced the Vietnam War, and the Cambodian genocide emerged from Sino–Soviet competition. The disputed reefs and islets of the South China Sea provide the most immediate potential flashpoint.

Indonesia, ASEAN's largest member state and likely to be one of the world's five largest economies by some measures in the next fifteen years, is central to Australia's future regional engagement. Ever since the Chifley government moved to support Indonesia's independence struggle after World War II, this has been a difficult relationship between two very different states. Confronting the challenge of developing a diverse population of 260 million people, many still close to the poverty line, in a porous archipelago, Indonesia looks inwards, eschewing alliances and seeking its security in the slow-flowing processes of multilateral institutions like the United Nations and ASEAN. Australia, in contrast, is anxious, outward-looking, activist and aligned.

Each country has put serious effort into understanding the other, and the record over the past fifty years is solid. But different priorities, miscalculation and self-centred decision-making have too often fogged the view, making the relationship vulnerable to sudden disruption. Deep public ignorance clouds popular understanding. Just 27 per cent of Australian respondents to the 2017 Lowy poll agreed that Indonesia was a democracy.

Generations of Australian policymakers and diplomats have worked hard to build bilateral relationships and regional institutions in South-East Asia, but Australia needs to lift its game again. South-East Asia's economies have recovered from the battering of the Asian financial crisis twenty years ago, but unresolved political tensions exist in a number of countries, including Thailand, Malaysia and Myanmar. Half the region's population of 620 million is under the age of thirty. In areas like the southern Philippines, young men are willing recruits for Islamist extremist groups.

South-East Asia is the part of the world whose importance to the emerging international system lines up most directly with Australia's capacity to craft and influence outcomes. The Turnbull government has made a promising start with its proposed summit meeting with the ASEAN states in 2018.

The Pacific

Largely ignored in the public debate, but imposing themselves insistently on the work of Australian foreign policymakers, are the island states of the South-West Pacific, ranging from Papua New Guinea to the tiny Pacific atolls. This region, too, is throwing up new challenges. Its vulnerability to climate change and extreme weather events greatly increases the risk of humanitarian disasters, to which Australia will have to respond. Australia's friends and allies expect it to bear the weight of helping in this part of the world. New Zealand is the other important player: Australia's policies in the South Pacific are almost always more effective when they are coordinated with Wellington's.

Australia's border with Papua New Guinea is less than four kilometres distant in the Torres Strait. PNG's population, already 7.6 million, and growing by more than 3 per cent a year, may reach Australia's current size by the middle of the century. It has rich mineral and other resources, but poor governance and increasing corruption meant that in 2016 PNG ranked just 154th on the United Nations Development Program's human development index and 136th in Transparency International's corruption perception index. Rates of infection of tuberculosis, HIV/AIDS and other diseases are rising. Maternal mortality rates are double those targeted in the United Nations' Millennium Development Goals. The average adult in PNG has had just four years of schooling, less than anywhere else in the region. Levels of crime and violence are rising.

In the South Pacific, Australian foreign policy directly encounters the tension between power and influence. Compared with the small island states, Australia has a great deal of power, but influence is much harder to exercise. Time after time, Canberra's capacity to get regional governments to do what it wants – whether restoring democracy in Fiji, or improving governance in PNG or on tiny Nauru – has turned out to be less than it hoped. The region tests Australia's skills in advocacy and persuasion more intensely than in most areas of foreign policy. From Melanesia to the small island states like Kiribati, the South Pacific provides an ongoing case study in how and where development assistance and humanitarian aid can make a difference.

The consequences of policy failure in the South Pacific, from easier operating conditions for transnational criminals to new disease outbreaks, will transmit themselves quickly to the Australian mainland.

Foreign policy in a new era

The change Australian foreign policy now faces is greater than any since that period when we realised that Britain could no longer sustain the role it had previously played in our defence or trade policies. But this transition will be harder for us. Fifty years ago, new markets in Japan and Korea were opening up to take up the economic slack, the United States was an obvious security partner, and as the Vietnam War ended and ASEAN was established, the Asian strategic environment looked less threatening. Now, no easy alternatives to our economic links with China exist. And far from looking more benign, the security outlook in East Asia is increasingly unpredictable.

This will be a world in which we are less able to rely on our traditional partners. Britain will no longer be an entry point for us to Europe and, after Brexit, will be less influential globally. And whatever follows the Trump administration, the United States is likely to be more focused on itself and less interested in terraforming the global landscape in its own image.

It is often claimed that Australia needs a more independent foreign policy. That's the wrong way of looking at it. Australia has had a sovereign identity in the world since 1942, when parliament belatedly declared Australia's sovereign identity by ratifying the Statute of Westminster. No one has forced us to fight particular wars or pursue particular goals. It was all our own doing. Calls for a more independent policy deflect responsibility for our own actions to others and help us evade the proper analysis of our own national mistakes. It's not independence that Australian foreign policy needs, but substance, subtlety and creativity.

Foreign policy can't carry this weight alone. The other elements of statecraft, and especially the strength of the economy, must play their part. But we need to invest in the institutions and instruments of Australian foreign policy – our overseas posts, our trained diplomats, our soft power potential to influence and encourage – with the same calculation that we invest in our defence capabilities. A robust, capable Department of Foreign Affairs and Trade is fundamental to Australia's global power and reach.

Foreign policy is not physics; it is ecology. It operates in – and on – an international environment of bewildering interdependence, whose qualities, like those of any complex adaptive system, are impossible to anticipate. So Australia's basic objective in the difficult time ahead should be to avoid cutting any options off, to diversify our markets and our partners, and to deepen our international engagement. In other words, to maximise the choices available to us at any given point, whatever circumstances arise.

Australia now needs to marshal its national resources in order to help construct the new order and protect what is important in the current one, just as it did in 1945 at the San Francisco conference. We will have to do a lot more work ourselves in forums like the United Nations and the World Trade Organization to preserve our interests. To defend what we want from the liberal order, we need to walk into the middle of the global arena with a large banner inscribed "global rules" and urge others to gather around. We must identify areas where opportunities exist to build coalitions of interest on new subjects – perhaps the control of lethal autonomous weapons (killer drones) or the rules governing genetic engineering.

To construct the new order in a world in which power is much more diffuse than in 1945, we need to broaden the company we keep – to seek more partners, wherever we can find them. Europe and some of the less-travelled byways of past Australian foreign policy, such as Latin America and Central Asia, will demand greater attention.

Australia faces a momentous national test in adjusting to these geopolitical changes. The good news is that the community seems up to it. Outside of wars, terrorist attacks and high-profile consular cases, foreign policy has not historically been of much interest to the public. But the world itself certainly is. Six million Australians were born overseas (a proportion of the population higher than for 120 years), a million or so are living, working or travelling abroad at any one time, and according to the 2017 Lowy poll, nearly four in five of us believe that globalisation is good for Australia. More than 600 submissions from individuals and groups, ranging from the Sydney Symphony Orchestra to the Football Federation of Australia, were delivered to the government's 2017 foreign policy white paper team. That's an important start.

Donald Trump may turn out to be an unexpected friend of the Australia–US relationship

Australians need to see themselves as the actors, not the audience, in the drama of the changing world; to shake off that nagging fear of abandonment and replace it with confidence in our capacity to set our own goals and to understand the path we have to make, with others or alone, to get there. No one else can do it for us. ∎

WHAT DOES CHINA WANT?

Xi Jinping
and the path
to greatness

Linda Jakobson

The mood in Canberra towards the People's Republic of China is souring. No single event has spurred this downward spiral; rather, a string of incidents and actions by the PRC have impelled many in Canberra to re-examine the Beijing government's pledge to rise peacefully. These include continuous media reports about the PRC government's efforts to meddle in Australian society, the PRC's insistence that it has every right to fortify artificial land features in the South China Sea, Beijing's retaliation against select South Korean industries to display its displeasure over Seoul's decision to deploy a US missile defence system, and the hardine speech by PRC President Xi Jinping on the twentieth anniversary of the Hong Kong handover. These have all chipped away at the image of a rising power that is genuinely committed to mutual respect among nations.

Of course, at the official level the relationship is fine. The comprehensive strategic partnership established in 2012 between the two countries is alive and well. The smiles and buoyant mood during Premier Li Keqiang's visit to Australia in March 2017 attest to this. But just below the surface there are numerous indications of a deteriorating relationship and increasing disagreement among Australian policymakers about the right way to engage with China. Protecting Australia's interests with effective responses to the PRC's actions – be they in the South and East China Seas or within Australian society – has never been more demanding.

To be effective, such responses will need to have as a starting point a clear sense of Australia's national interests with regard to the PRC. Australian decision-makers also need to have a clear grasp of the national interests of modern-day China in the minds of its leaders. The driving forces behind the ambitions of the Communist Party of China (CPC) are intertwined with a historic longing for greatness, which unites rulers and citizens.

Geography defines destiny. Just as Australia's sense of vulnerability stems from its geography and a "fear of abandonment" by its security guarantor, Chinese strategic anxiety is shaped by a fear of encirclement. In the PRC's view, the United States has flourished in part because of its benign environment. If China were situated where the United States is and had but two friendly neighbours, it would not be concerned about encirclement. Instead, hostile adversaries from overland or across the sea have contributed to the collapse of Chinese dynasties over millennia.

Chinese strategic culture is also shaped by a preoccupation with legitimacy. Confucian thought stipulated that the right to rule – the Mandate of Heaven – was bestowed upon virtuous rulers. It was – and still is – impossible to know when a dynasty loses this mandate and collapses, only that such a fate befalls unjust rulers. The existential anxiety of today's leaders of the CPC, regardless of the PRC's recent resurgence of power, arises from a fear that the Party is losing its legitimacy. Behind closed doors they acknowledge that the Soviet Communist Party collapsed because it lacked legitimacy in the minds of the Soviet peoples. Chinese senior officials are haunted by this example, not to mention the fate of Romania's Nicolae Ceaușescu (executed by his own citizens).

The need for those in power to provide security while maintaining legitimacy – however defined – is one of the key factors that need to be considered when answering the question: what does China want?

But, first, one must define China. Are we talking about "China," the civilisation for which not only over 1.3 billion citizens of the People's Republic of China feel a deep affinity, but also most of the over 50 million people of Chinese heritage who are citizens of other countries? Are we referring only to the citizens of the PRC? Or does China stand for the CPC, which in 1949 founded this one-party authoritarian state? This is not a quibble about semantics, but fundamental to understanding the complexities of China's ambition. People of Chinese heritage universally, PRC citizens included, and the Party all desire certain things – respect, for example. But even then, they would disagree on the methods and pathways to gain respect.

The more assertive China becomes, the more important it is to distinguish between CPC ambition and the emotional pull that people of Chinese heritage feel towards their cultural roots. In Canberra, officials and commentators alike would do well to use the words "China" and "Chinese" more prudently. Why not speak of the People's Republic of China, or PRC, when we mean the state that calls itself just that?

This essay primarily explores the question of what China wants from the viewpoint of the CPC leadership. After all, it is predominantly the decisions the Party makes which will affect the PRC's future and that of the Asia-Pacific region. Concerns about the Party's intentions loom large when Australians discuss possible PRC threats to national security, the rule of law, sovereignty and the Australian way of life.

To seem indispensable

The communist leaders of the PRC have an overriding existential desire: to stay in power. Some would say that this is true of politicians the world over, regardless of the political system. In some regards it is, but in the PRC there is no mechanism such as an election to cast aside one party, nor is there an alternative political party to turn to if the current one is deemed incompetent or unwanted.

Moreover, in the PRC the ruling party uses brute force to deter the emergence of any opposition to its rule. Voices of dissent are quashed.

The internet and media of all types are controlled. Citizens of the PRC are constantly reminded that the demise of the Party would mean political upheaval, with all the associated risks of instability. In the CPC's narrative of history, this leads to weakness, division of the country and, inevitably, the suffering of ordinary people. After the Soviet Union disintegrated, the PRC media focused on the social havoc that ensued, especially its effect on ordinary Russians. In Chinese, the expression "to walk the Soviet road" became synonymous with "chaos."

Of the core interests the Party publicly acknowledges, upholding the socialist system – keeping the CPC in power – is routinely mentioned first. Territorial integrity and upholding sovereignty comes second, followed by ensuring sustainable economic development.

The Party is desperate to instil in the citizenry a sense of its own indispensability. In public statements, propaganda officials emphasise that it is thanks to the Party that China is united, that living standards are improving, that China is now respected, and that China's national strength, however measured, is rising. For example, in August Xi Jinping, marking the ninetieth anniversary of the founding of the People's Liberation Army (PLA), said:

> Over these ninety years, our country and our people have experienced setbacks and advances, suffering and glory. We have witnessed unprecedented historical change, and realised the great leap from standing up to growing wealthy and strong. This is the victory of the strong CPC leadership, it is the victory of the

Chinese people's unremitting struggles, and it is also the victory of the courageous People's Liberation Army.

Xi and his peers have every reason to feel jittery about losing power. Marxist-Leninist thought does not capture the imagination of PRC citizens; getting rich does. Economic growth has been the bedrock of the Party's legitimacy since 1978, when the PRC did an about-turn and embraced the policies of Deng Xiaoping's reform and opening. Hundreds of millions of people have been lifted out of poverty; nearly 300 million people have moved into the middle and wealthy classes. Rising living standards have led to an expectation that the upward trajectory will continue. But economic growth is slowing. The next wave of necessary reforms to restructure the economy will infringe upon the benefits of privileged interest groups that are essential to the Party's grip on power. Therefore, Xi dithers and to date has not summoned the political courage to embark on genuine restructuring, as was envisioned in the ambitious sixty-point reform agenda in 2013, one year after he took the helm.

Xi and his peers have every reason to feel jittery about losing power

At the same time, respect for the Party has declined considerably, both among elites and ordinary people, because of rampant corruption and nepotism among Party members. Xi Jinping is intent on restoring the authority of the Party. He has overseen a ferocious anti-corruption campaign that has lasted longer than any previous one. He sprinkles references to both revolutionary Mao Zedong thought and ancient Confucian thought through his speeches, insisting that Party members need to be morally upright model citizens. He has not only ordered ideological education to be strengthened in schools and state-run workplaces, he has also created new CPC entities to ensure that the Party, not the government, is in firm control of key decisions.

When Xi Jinping became leader of the CPC in late 2012, he set as his goal the "great rejuvenation of the Chinese nation" and embraced the "China Dream" as his signature slogan. There is much in common with Donald Trump's aspiration to "make America great again": more jobs, more respect, a return to military greatness. As with the American version, which had been promoted by Ronald Reagan more than two decades earlier, the China Dream had been discussed for a decade or so whenever Party ideologues debated how to justify policies with something other than tired Marxist-Leninist slogans.

To be wealthy and powerful

Understanding the motivations and undercurrents behind Xi Jinping's China Dream is essential to understanding what China – defined as the CPC leadership – wants. Officially, the China Dream has four parts: Strong China (economically, politically, diplomatically, scientifically, militarily); Civilised China (equity and fairness, rich culture, high morals); Harmonious China (amity among social classes); and Beautiful China (healthy environment, low pollution). In reality, the China Dream is shorthand for Xi Jinping's ambition to restore the ideological legitimacy and attractiveness of the Party by making China wealthy and powerful. He wants to boost the self-esteem of all Chinese, but especially Party members. Otherwise, CPC members in China may face the same fate as their Soviet or Romanian comrades.

The objectives of the China Dream are stated in the "Two Centenary Goals: "comprehensively build a moderately prosperous society," defined as doubling 2010 GDP and per capita income by 2021 (the year the CPC celebrates its 100th birthday), and to "build a modern socialist country that is prosperous, strong, democratic, culturally advanced and harmonious" by 2049 (the centenary of the People's Republic of China).

Senior leaders know the Party must continue to raise the living standards of PRC citizens. This alone is a gargantuan task. Despite China's rapid growth, its booming international trade and expanding overseas assets, it is worth considering that only one-fifth of the population – that is, 260 million people – are considered middle-class, while 150 million Chinese still live in extreme poverty (under US$1.90 per day) and a staggering 360 million live on less than US$3.10 per day.

Though maintaining economic growth is essential to keeping the CPC in power, it alone will not suffice. The China Dream encapsulates a historical yearning for wealth, power, respect and global standing. But there is a difference between the emphasis the Party places on one

type of historic narrative and a distinct and deep historical consciousness that is shared by many, if not most people of Chinese heritage,
regardless of their nationality.

"YanHuang ZiSun" (炎黃子孫) – descendants of the legendary
Fiery and Yellow emperors – is a neutral term to describe all people
of Han Chinese heritage. A common trait is a keen awareness of the
uniquely long history of uninterrupted Chinese civilisation and cultural achievement which makes them an exceptional people. Whereas
American exceptionalism is imbued with the energy of "the new,"
Chinese exceptionalism draws upon "the old" – from its over five millennia as a distinct civilisation. In casual conversation educated people
of Chinese ethnicity, regardless of their nationality, regularly draw
historic parallels using allegories and sayings with which the Chinese
language is rich. When speaking of a person who has overestimated
himself or herself, it is common to say, "He presents himself as a master at the door of Lu Ban," a legendary master craftsman, called the
father of Chinese carpentry. "When the lips are gone, the teeth will be
cold" is a saying from a well-known story about the interdependence
of two adjacent states from China's antiquity. Military leader Zhu De
used it during the Korean War to stress that without North Korea as
a buffer, the PRC would be exposed to invasion. Until recently, PRC
commentators still described Beijing's relationship with Pyongyang
with the expression "as close as lips and teeth."

The Chinese understanding of time also tends to differ from
Western concepts. Whereas linear interpretations of history are the

Western norm, the Chinese assess history based on recurring patterns. This cyclical understanding of history is exemplified in the opening words of the classical novel *Romance of the Three Kingdoms*: "The empire, long divided, must unite; long united, must divide. Thus it has ever been." Dynasties rise and fall, but Chinese civilisation endures. In private conversation, CPC officials and ordinary citizens alike allude to a presumption that the People's Republic constitutes just one cycle in Chinese history and so is destined to one day lose the Mandate of Heaven.

To redress the history of victimhood

The CPC's narrative about history certainly emphasises China's remarkable culture and civilisation. However, it is obsessed with the "century of humiliation," approximately from the 1840s to the 1940s. The same message has been drummed into the consciousness of every person educated in the PRC since 1949: Chinese people suffered horribly at the hands of outsiders, especially Japan and the Western powers – which indeed they did. China was subjugated by outsiders because it was weak, and the Party is to be thanked for making China strong again. (This too is a reasonable statement, though it is first and foremost PRC citizens who deserve credit for the achievement.)

An elaborate tapestry of humiliation and shame is part of the national psyche. It creates troubling undercurrents and inhibits the formation of a neutral view of other countries. Most every nation has a period of history that evokes shame, but in many countries the painful period is addressed, a more constructive national narrative gradually becomes the norm, and the nation moves on. In the PRC, the century of humiliation continues to hold immense emotional sway over citizens because the Party reminds them of the abysmal state of the nation during that period and its role in ending it. The century of humiliation is the focus of a constant stream of new books, articles, musicals, television dramas, art exhibitions and even theme parks. To quote academic Zheng Wang, it is a "lasting trauma seared into the national consciousness."

This legacy of victimhood colours the way PRC citizens, including policymakers, view the outside world and how the PRC should interact with other states. Corruption within the bureaucracy and widespread addiction to opium have been pinpointed as reasons for the Chinese empire's demise at the hands of foreigners: hence the CPC campaigns to promote strong and healthy citizens and improve moral standards.

The longing for greatness is not Xi's invention. It was Jiang Zemin who first promoted the "great rejuvenation of the Chinese nation." For most citizens, that translates into the necessity that the PRC be strong. The vast majority of PRC citizens agree with Xi's vision – and that of the leaders before him – that the PRC should strive for wealth, power and greatness.

Efforts to rapidly construct a modern naval force, for example, are driven by the vulnerability the PRC feels in its near waters. The century of humiliation and fear of foreign encirclement also in part explain Beijing's insistence on its territorial claims in the South

China Sea. Senior Australian security officials have said that China has already achieved its goal of creating a buffer zone through the construction of facilities on man-made features in the South China Sea. To the PRC government and citizens, any concessions made in disputed waters would compromise the PRC's territorial integrity, and would be akin to surrendering Hong Kong to the British Empire or allowing foreign concessions in Shanghai. The Party's spokespeople and social media campaigns alike emphasise that during the first decades of reform the PRC was passive and watched idly as its interests were encroached on by other claimants. Now that the nation's strength has been restored, there is the need to "not yield a single inch of dirt" of PRC territory.

Xi has built up enormous expectations by his words and actions about China's role in the region

The spotlight on the century of humiliation also sensitises PRC citizens to any hint of their country being mistreated or belittled on the international stage. All affronts to the PRC's national dignity must be met with a strong response. PRC netizens bemoan the way their nation is still "bullied" by smaller countries such as Vietnam and the Philippines in international courts, despite its far greater military strength. They also complain about their submissive and weak leaders. In a reflection of the imperial tributary system mindset, nationalist commentary includes claims that China is a "big country" and all neighbouring states are "small countries" that must pay due deference.

There is also an insecurity, never articulated in public but some-times in private, which stems from the acknowledgement that democratic nations will not respect the PRC until there is more transparency and accountability in the political system and before human rights abuses are drastically curbed. Even then, private views among educated citizens of the PRC about the desirability of a more pluralistic political system have become far less certain over the past decade. The global financial crisis, continuous terrorist attacks in Europe, mass shootings in the United States and the rise of populist politicians, culminating in Trump's election victory, have all seriously undermined the appeal of parliamentary democracy.

PRC citizens are no different from any other people in their feel-ings of pride for their country. They are proud of numerous artistic creations and technological inventions over the millennia; proud of the name "Middle Kingdom," which places China at the centre of the universe; and proud of the PRC's immense accomplishments over the past four decades of modernisation. But the ongoing reminders by pro-paganda officials of the "historical hurts," as historian Ian Buruma has called these affronts, increasingly brings to the fore an explosive type of nationalism, which seeks to wipe out the humiliations of the past.

To lead the region

Besides staying in power, the CPC aspires for the PRC to lead Indo-Pacific Asia. But India, Japan and the United States will make sure that for at least some time to come, decades even, it does not lead the region alone. The ambition, goals and behaviour of the PRC, India, Japan and the United States will shape the region, and to an extent the international system.

Xi Jinping and his colleagues will have to continuously balance between providing security and ensuring legitimacy. A peaceful environment is imperative if the PRC is to continue to modernise. Xi wants to go down in history as a transformative leader. As the son of a well-known revolutionary leader, he is viewed in China as the CPC flag-bearer and trailblazer of the twenty-first century. He has worked for the Party his entire life. He had extensive experience in demanding leadership positions, among others as a provincial Party secretary, before he was appointed in 2007 to the CPC Politburo Standing Committee. To make China great again, Xi must summon the political courage to reform the economy, a risk-laden process, as it could endanger domestic political stability. He also needs peace on China's borders.

On the other hand, the PRC's leaders simply cannot risk being perceived as weak by the people. Xi has built up enormous expectations by his actions and words about China's role in the region and its military strength, especially on maritime sovereignty issues. CPC emphasis on past victimhood and the increased capabilities of the PLA strengthens a nationalist mindset. Because the leaders are insecure about their political legitimacy, propaganda officials tend to have a knee-jerk reaction to actions or statements by outsiders that are deemed confronting.

No one can say with certainty how the PRC will use its power in the years ahead. There are scores of examples from the past few years, which point to a PRC tendency to ignore international rules and use coercion when it does not get its way. Less noticed are the scores of examples which point to a PRC that abides by the rules and norms of the international order. These rules are all ones that the PRC had no hand in shaping.

There are also scores of examples of other great powers that bully smaller states and disregard decisions by international courts. Throughout history, a rising power has always demanded adjustments to rules that it deemed threatening to its national interests.

Canberra faces a genuine conundrum. Australian senior officials and government ministers repeatedly acknowledge the right of the Beijing government to have more say in regional affairs. But then they hasten to add that this must take place according to the rules-based order that underpins security and prosperity in the region. No one spells out that this rules-based order is the one that the PRC had no role in shaping, only that it is the order that Australia deems as advantageous for Australia.

For example, last June, in his first major foreign policy address as prime minister, Malcolm Turnbull said that the PRC will play a larger role in shaping the region, and that it is natural that Beijing will seek strategic influence to match its economic weight. He added: "We want to see China fill the leadership role it desires in a way which strengthens the regional order that has served us all so well." Here, precisely, is the conundrum. This "regional order" is the one established and dominated by the United States and underpinned by its military power. Australia accepts that change is in the air, but refrains from acknowledging that the change will probably happen in ways that are not favourable to its own interests. The regional order with the United States as the prime security guarantor is not the regional order the PRC wants any longer.

At the same time, we do not know what kind of an order Xi Jinping aspires to. He has said that Asians should be responsible for security in Asia. He has spoken of a community of common destiny. But the PRC knows full well – and officials acknowledge this in private – that China relies on the United States to constrain a surge of Japanese nationalism which could lead to a nasty rivalry between Japan and China. The US role is pivotal, but what kind of role it could have in a China-dominated region is unclear. The unpredictability and unreliability of the Trump administration's Asia policies make Australia's predicament even bleaker.

How Australia should respond to what China wants

Australian prosperity is dependent on the PRC in a way that simply cannot be ignored. Australia cannot kill the golden goose that keeps on giving. Despite enormous problems, including the reluctance of special interest groups to accept reform of state-owned enterprises, a rapidly ageing population and severe environmental degradation, the projected growth of the Chinese middle class is staggering. On moderate estimates, it will grow from 12 per cent of the population in 2009 to 73 per cent in 2030; that is, 850 million people.

Alarm about the PRC's intentions and what they mean for Australia is especially palpable among the security establishment in Canberra. It seems as if each news report describing China's unsavoury actions is greeted with the muttered words, "I told you so." As if those who view Australia's relationship with the PRC through a mostly black lens were the only ones who ever understood the extreme challenges of dealing with an undemocratic, authoritarian but increasingly influential state.

Never before has it been more important for Australia to find ways to build on its strategic comprehensive partnership with the PRC. Getting closer does not mean cosying up. Understanding the aims and also the policies of the PRC is paramount. Only then can Australia have any hope of exerting influence on China's policy choices – either alone or preferably with regional leaders such as Indonesia. Australian policymakers should know their PRC counterparts as well as they know their American ones. This will require enormous effort. There is no question that protecting Australian interests as the PRC's ambitions grow will be an ever-increasing challenge for Canberra.

Australia also needs to devote greater resources to forging close ties in the region. Australia already invests considerably in its relationships with Indonesia, Japan, South Korea and India. But Australia's ability to work with these four countries, as well as with the PRC, will determine Australia's future. So if resources that facilitate meaningful, across-the-board engagement are scarce, as they often are, extensive funds should be channelled selectively – and only to these five.

Perhaps the most complex challenge for Australia's political leaders and public servants will be to rationally manage efforts by PRC officials to interfere in discussions about the PRC within Australia. Sometimes the attempts are part of legitimate public diplomacy. Sometimes the attempts confront freedom of speech and academic freedom, or occur indirectly with the help of students or other PRC citizens.

Recent media reports about these efforts have caused jitters among Chinese Australians. Xenophobic reactions or finger pointing risk tearing apart social cohesion.

Xi strikes a chord beyond the borders of the PRC when he speaks about China's rich cultural heritage. Overseas Chinese, including Chinese Australians, are proud of that heritage too. This can cause conflicting emotions in those who do not feel an attachment to the PRC or those who abhor some of the policies of the PRC but still honour their Chinese cultural heritage. Many Chinese Australians also take issue with the Australian media's relentless criticism of the PRC; they find it emotionally taxing to hear the country of their ancestors being badmouthed, even if they agree with some or even much of the criticism. Furthermore, even those who characterise themselves as "no friend of the CPC" wish that fellow Australians would understand that the CPC deserves credit for overseeing the dramatic and positive transformation of the past forty years.

Australians of Chinese heritage today number approximately 1 million. The contributions of the diverse Chinese-Australian communities to Australian society should not be overlooked. Senior government ministers should articulate this in a high-profile public setting. In the present climate, Chinese Australians or PRC nationals who are permanent residents feel targeted by the media and the mainstream Australian population at large. In particular, those PRC-born Australians who cherish Australian values and condemn attempts by Chinese international students to curb academic freedom in Australian universities worry that they will be viewed as "stooges of the CPC." In turn, Australians of Chinese heritage who are not from the PRC complain of the same anxieties, because they feel all people of Chinese background are viewed as one.

From hardline speeches by Xi, the military parades celebrating the PLA's ninetieth anniversary and shows of strength from the PLA Navy in China's maritime vicinity, it is evident that Xi is doing his best to lay the groundwork for the PRC to one day assume the dominant position in the region. How disruptive the push-and-pull becomes between China and the rest of the region – and between China and the United States, in particular, as China seeks to increase its sway in Indo-Pacific Asia – will define peace in the region.

Australia will be part of that push-and-pull. Maintaining a fruitful and constructive relationship with the PRC in all its dimensions is the biggest challenge Australia has ever faced. ∎

The author is grateful to Jackson Kwok, research assistant at China Matters. This article draws on parts of an unpublished briefing paper that the author and Kwok co-authored, which included an assessment of China's ambition.

THE CHANGING FACE OF AUSTRALIA

Completing the shift
to a Eurasian nation

George Megalogenis

The new China migrant

One of the intriguing chores of newspaper journalism involves finding a case study to accompany a broader story about who we are as a nation. The family or individual selected to illustrate the piece carries a heavy burden: to embody a social trend.

When the 2011 census revealed that our national identity was evolving from Anglo-European to Eurasian, I had little trouble convincing my editors at the *Australian* to illustrate that shift with a Chinese family. I thought – wrongly – that it didn't really matter when our avatars migrated to Australia. The key point to my mind was that they lived in Sydney, where the data showed the Chinese-born were poised to replace the English-born as the city's largest migrant community. Nationally, Mandarin had already overtaken Italian as the second-most common language spoken after English. Our front page scoop, published in 2012, featured a Chinese Australian family from Epping, in Sydney's north-west. It was a gorgeous image: the Chinese parents and their Australian-born children getting ready for their day. The two girls, in their private-school uniforms, were finishing breakfast as Mum and Dad shared a joke with them. This family's journey from China to Australia's cosmopolitan heartland seemed to reaffirm the essential virtue of our migration program. "The Sydney couple moved from China to Australia in 1990 with little money to start with, and for the next four years both worked up to 90 hours a week in various jobs until they had saved enough to buy their own business," the article read. "More than two decades later, the couple run a successful chain of health food stores across the city, and employ 23 Australian workers."

After the release of the 2016 census, I reread this article and kicked myself. The case study was misleading. Our Chinese-Australian family represented the twentieth-century story of migration, not the twenty-first. They had followed the familiar two-generation path from outsiders to middle class. The parents left a damaged nation and put down roots in Australia through home ownership and small business, while their children outperformed their peers at school and then in the professions. The continuity with previous waves of migrants from southern Europe and Asia was easy to see.

When the couple moved to Australia in 1990, China was a poor nation in transition. Its economy was only 30 per cent the size of Italy's and 12 per cent the size of Japan's. The mistake I made was to assume continuity between the Chinese migrants of the 1980s and '90s and those who have arrived since 2001, after China's entry into the World Trade Organization. That was the pivotal event which transformed the global economy in China's favour. It marks the dividing line between old and new China. In 1990, China was the eleventh-largest economy in the world; two decades later, it was the second-largest.

The typical twenty-first-century migrant from China skips the first generation of struggle. They land between the middle class and the richest either as a tertiary student or a skilled worker. Their wealth and power come from who they were in China, not what they become in Australia. And this presents a dilemma for policymakers in Australia, because Beijing views its twenty-first-century emigrants as an extension of their state. As departing Secretary of Defence Dennis Richardson explained in his farewell address in May this year, "It is no secret that the Chinese government keeps a watchful eye inside Australian Chinese communities and effectively controls some Chinese language media in Australia."

An Australia with two big Eurasian capitals cannot continue to behave as a white outpost in Asia

As a migration optimist, I suspect that Beijing's monitoring will be counterproductive, driving the new arrivals into the arms of Australia's extended multicultural family. But policymakers should not underestimate the unique circumstances at play. This is the first time in Australia's

229-year settler history that the elites of a rising nation have come here with their mother country keeping a "watchful eye" on them.

The numbers involved are significant. Australia had settled 143,000 migrants from old China by 2001. In just fifteen years, the migrants from new China have trebled that total to more than 500,000.

The migrants of new China are not the only group that differ from previous waves from the same country. The Indian migrants of the twenty-first century also carry the elevated expectations of a rising nation, although without the baggage of one-party state surveillance. Like the Chinese, the Indians are younger and better educated than their compatriots who migrated in the 1980s and '90s.

These Chinese and Indian migrants are the vanguard of a migration boom that is unleashing the most profound changes to Australian society since the gold rushes of the 1850s. Every aspect of policy will be affected.

Australia's economic fortunes have been tied to Asia since 1966–67, when Japan replaced the United Kingdom as the number one destination for our exports. But our demography had been a decade behind this engagement. The first substantial wave of Asian migration did not arrive until the Vietnamese refugees were received in large numbers in the late 1970s.

China's rise has fused trade and demography. China replaced Japan as our biggest customer in 2009–10, and the Chinese-born replaced the English-born as the largest migrant community in Sydney in 2011.

To paraphrase Paul Keating, our future is not only in Asia, it is Eurasian.

Australia's outlook on the region, and the world, will inevitably adapt with its ethnic mix. This will require a new compact to address the mismatch between our demography and our political institutions. Our parliament remains much whiter than the nation it serves. Our businesses happily trade with Asia, while locking the boardroom door to Asian Australians. And our foreign policy remains rooted in an Anglo past, with the default question being to ask the Americans, "How can we help?"

This essay is a call to arms to elevate migration to a first-order concern for foreign affairs to help us complete the transition to a Eurasian nation that is bound neither to the aspirations of our largest trading partner, China, nor to the anxieties of our ally, the United States. The first step is to understand who we are.

Australia divided

Australia's identity is undergoing an epic transformation. In seventy short years, we have shifted from being the most insular rich nation on Earth to being a global role model for diversity. It took fifty years to get from white to Anglo-European, but only another twenty to cross the threshold to Eurasian.

When the door was first opened to mass migration, in 1947, nine out of ten Australians were born locally, and of those who were migrants, the English accounted for half. The last time the English represented the majority of the migrants living in Australia was in December 1788, when Indigenous Australians numbered as many as 1 million, while the settler population was 859.

By 1976, 20 per cent of the Australian population had been born overseas, and almost half were from Europe (8 per cent of the total population). That year, the Asian-born were the new minority, at 1 per cent of the total population.

The initial Asian wave, led by Vietnam in the late 1970s and then by China and the Philippines in the 1980s, was not as big as the postwar wave from Europe. But it laid the foundation for Australia's population to shift to a more Eurasian composition, as migration from the region accelerated with the rise of China and India in the twenty-first century.

People born overseas now make up more than 28 per cent of the total Australian population – a level not seen since the 1890s. More than a third of these are from Asia. Add the local-born with at least one parent who was a migrant, and just under half the total population is either first- or second-generation Australian.

Now, the rub. This national snapshot conceals dramatic variations between the states. The affluent south-east corner of the continent and the west can be counted as majority new Australian: in Western Australia, Victoria, New South Wales and the ACT, the first and second generations combine to form more than half the population. But in the rest of the country, old Australia dominates. In Tasmania, the first and second generations are just 25.6 per cent of the state's population; in the Northern Territory, they are 37.9 per cent; Queensland, 41 per cent; and South Australia, 44.5 per cent. Each capital city has a particular ethnic make-up that bears only passing resemblance to that of the nation at large. It is in these differences that the multiple opportunities and challenges of mass skilled migration can be best understood.

The following is a quick tour around Australia, from its most diverse to its whitest population centres. The findings, drawn from customised census data supplied by the Australian Bureau of Statistics, underline how quickly the nation is being separated into a series of distinct cultural identities.

Our journey begins in Newcastle, the only city or town in which the top five migrant communities are in the same order as the nation as a whole: the English-born first, the New Zealanders second, Chinese third, Indians fourth and Filipinos fifth.

To the north, the populations of the Gold Coast and Brisbane are unique. There, New Zealanders are the largest migrant community, and South Africans are in the top five, ahead of people from the Philippines.

Travel a little further north and you arrive at Australia's whitest population centre, the Sunshine Coast, where the Chinese and Indians are not even in the top five. Here the English-born are first, New Zealanders second, South Africans third, Germans fourth and Americans fifth.

Now on to Darwin, where two twentieth-century migration waves meet. Filipinos are the largest migrant community, and the Greeks are still in the top five, just ahead of the Chinese.

Birth place of residents, based on author's analysis of ABS Census 2016 data

AUSTRALIA	%	SYDNEY	%	MELBOURNE	%
Australia	71.7	Australia	60.9	Australia	63.9
England	4.2	China	5.0	India	3.8
New Zealand	2.4	England	3.4	China	3.7
China	2.3	India	2.9	England	3.2
India	2.1	New Zealand	1.9	Vietnam	1.9
Phillippines	1.1	Vietnam	1.8	New Zealand	1.9
Vietnam	1.0	Phillippines	1.7	Italy	1.5
Italy	0.8	Lebanon	1.2	Sri Lanka	1.3
South Africa	0.7	South Korea	1.1	Malaysia	1.1
Malaysia	0.6	Hong Kong	0.9	Greece	1.1

BRISBANE	%	PERTH	%	ADELAIDE	%
Australia	72.2	Australia	61.4	Australia	72.2
New Zealand	5.0	England	9.2	England	6.6
England	4.2	New Zealand	3.4	India	2.1
China	1.7	India	2.6	China	2.0
India	1.7	South Africa	1.9	Italy	1.4
South Africa	1.0	Malaysia	1.6	Vietnam	1.1
Phillippines	1.0	China	1.4	Phillippines	0.8
Vietnam	0.8	Phillippines	1.4	New Zealand	0.8
South Korea	0.6	Italy	1.0	Germany	0.7
Malaysia	0.5	Ireland	0.9	Greece	0.7

HOBART	%	DARWIN	%	CANBERRA	%
Australia	85.3	Australia	71.1	Australia	72.0
England	3.8	Phillippines	4.1	England	4.0
China	1.1	England	3.5	China	3.0
New Zealand	0.9	New Zealand	2.4	India	2.8
India	0.6	India	2.2	New Zealand	1.3
Germany	0.5	Greece	1.0	Phillippines	1.0
United States	0.4	China	0.9	Vietnam	0.9
South Africa	0.4	Indonesia	0.8	United States	0.7
Malaysia	0.4	Ireland	0.7	Sri Lanka	0.7
Netherlands	0.4	Vietnam	0.6	Malaysia	0.6

Perth is cut from another era again. The English are at the very top, and will likely remain there for some decades to come. Nationally, the English-born are 4.2 per cent of the population; in Perth, they are 9.2 per cent, and much younger than their kin on the eastern seaboard.

Adelaide is also very English – 6.6 per cent of the city's population. On the other hand, Hobart is relatively more Asian than might be expected. There, the Chinese are second behind the English, and ahead of the New Zealanders.

What these snapshots reveal is an Australia of genuine diversity. But it is in Melbourne and Sydney that we see the greatest changes.

In Melbourne, those born in India now form the largest migrant group, with the Chinese-born second. In Sydney, the Chinese are first and the Indians are on track to take second place before the end of the decade. Migration helps shape the character of each city. What will challenge policy makers and politicians is the economic and cultural separation of our two largest cities from the rest of the country. Melbourne and Sydney account for almost 40 per cent of the nation's population, but 75 per cent of the Chinese-born and 64 per cent of the Indian-born populations.

The scale and content of the migrant program since 2001 has shifted the Australian horizon, from what threatened to become a small, ageing nation to a top ten world economy. Consider the path Australia would have taken if the smaller intakes of the 1990s had been repeated in the first decades of the twenty-first century. Then, the fastest-growing state was Queensland – but this was a warning of stagnation rather than a sign of renewal. It was thought that Queensland would replace Victoria as the nation's second-largest state by the middle of the century, while the national population would stall at 26 million. A whiter Australia by default, not design. The estimate for the middle of the century is now at 38 million, and it may go even higher. Those additional residents will gravitate towards the two global cities unless federal and state governments intervene to promote decentralisation. On present trends, Melbourne will replace Sydney as the nation's largest city within the next twenty or thirty years.

This may not come to pass, of course. But the cultural shift is already underway and foreign policy has to adapt. An Australia with two big Eurasian capitals cannot continue to behave as a white outpost in Asia. There is a paradox at play here. Australia has to be more assertive and less offensive. By all means, remain America's best friend, but remember that our interests don't depend on the United States retaining its status as the world's largest economy. The US may genuinely believe that a trade war with China will keep it on top. But history tells us that the Australian economy performs best when the global economy is open.

The Chinese, on the other hand, may see an open global economy as a temporary phase before they rewrite the rules in their favour. That future is no more palatable for Australia than a US-led descent to protectionism.

To keep our region and the global economy open, Australia needs the goodwill of its neighbours. Indonesia, for instance, is on the cusp of becoming a top ten economy. Jakarta would be more inclined to run a joint ticket for openness with Australia if we can resist the impulse to continue seeing the relationship through the narrow domestic lens of asylum-seeker policy.

Hunting for a migrant scapegoat

Australia's political system is playing a dangerous game with migration. We have a gold standard migration program but a political debate that has more in common with the White Australia era of racial selection and sectarianism. The reality of the program is that we are settling twice as many migrants in the twenty-first century as we did in the twentieth. But the political rhetoric of border protection and tougher citizenship testing is sending a dangerous message, both domestically and abroad, of Australian retreat.

There was a time when this approach might have made short-term sense. It allowed John Howard to double the intake of migrants while assuring conservative voters that the back door remained bolted to asylum seekers. But once the scale and content of the migration program was revolutionised, the main parties had an obligation to educate and engage the electorate.

Howard's reform to the migration program ranks alongside the float of the dollar and the removal of the tariff wall. These all affect every aspect of Australian life: where we live, how we work and relate to one other, and our place in the world. Most contemporary politicians should be familiar with the numbers – the doubling of the annual intake from 80,000 at the turn of the twenty-first century to 190,000 today; the heavy bias towards skills over family reunion; the overwhelming majority of new arrivals winding up in Sydney or Melbourne. It's the implications they struggle with.

The key point to appreciate is that our diversity has accelerated over the past fifteen years. John Howard is primarily responsible for this, because he shifted the emphasis of the migration program from family reunion to skills. Initially, he did this while cutting the total intake – so it can't be said that the reform, when it was first introduced, was designed to create a big Australia. It just happened to work out that way once China began its rise, and our economy collected the double bonus of a resources and skilled migration boom. In 2000–01, the final year of Howard's migrant sceptic phase, the intake was 80,597, of which 56 per cent came via the skilled stream. If Australia had a recession in 2001, as most of the rich world did at the time, then the annual intake would have been dialled down. But we missed that recession, and Howard's demand-driven migration program kicked into a gear he had not anticipated.

As the economy roared in the early years of the twenty-first century, employers ran out of local workers and had to look overseas to fill the shortages. State governments also entered the marketplace for migrants, recruiting for their health and education systems. In 2007–08, the final year for which Howard was responsible, the intake was a record 158,630, of which 68 per cent were skilled.

There was little or no pushback from conservative voters or trade unions at the time. Migrants were not seen to be taking local jobs, because local-born Australians were enjoying the fruits of the mining, property and consumer booms. It is what happened after the global financial crisis – the recession we didn't have – that has tested public support for mass skilled migration. The intake set a new record level, even as the economy slowed, creating the misleading impression that the new arrivals must have taken jobs that would otherwise have gone to locals. In 2012–13 the intake surged again, to a new record of 190,000, where it has remained ever since. Skilled migrants continues to account for two-thirds of this elevated intake.

Yet the unemployment rate remains uncomfortably higher than it was before the GFC. Why bring in so many migrants when jobs are harder to find? It's a fair question for politicians to ask. But it does them no credit if they won't embrace the answer. Our population is ageing, and local-born job seekers are barely replacing those who retire each year. Therefore, employers and governments continue to look overseas to cover the skills gap, even though the economy is weaker in 2017 than it was in 2007.

The demand-driven model for migration has replaced mining as the main driver of domestic growth. This is a terrific story to tell, if only politics would take the time to appreciate the benefits.

What we have endured, instead, is a relentless search for a migrant scapegoat. Asylum seekers were an easy target while the boats were coming. But since the boats stopped, the finger of suspicion has been pointed at people who came here at our invitation. Prime ministers on both sides have been guilty of playing this game. Julia Gillard set the precedent in 2013 when she promised to "stop foreign workers being put at the front of the queue with Australian workers at the back." Her beef was with the temporary work visa program, not any individual community. Tony Abbott had no qualms in singling out a particular group: he questioned the loyalty of Muslim Australians.

Before he was prime minister, Malcolm Turnbull had been critical of both subtle and overt attacks on Australian multiculturalism. When he toppled Abbott in 2015, it seemed as if a reset button had been hit, returning us to the open Australia era of Whitlam, Fraser, Hawke and Keating. But Turnbull found himself caught in a pincer of parochialism. Opposition leader Bill Shorten stepped up Labor's attack on the 457 visa program, while conservative MPs pushed for a tougher citizenship test. Earlier this year, Turnbull bowed to both sides, promising to put "Australian workers first" and demanding that migrants embrace Australian values.

This new approach from Turnbull undermines public confidence in the migration program. He should have defended the temporary work visa program as an important feeder into the regular migration program. Half of all the migrants who are now granted permanent residency are sourced onshore: that is, they were already here on student or work visas and were recruited as permanent skilled workers.

If there is an issue with the model, it is the licence that deregulation gives employers to exploit migrant workers. Not all employers take advantage; most don't, because they cannot afford the reputational damage of exposure. But it is the abuses that attract attention. And in an age of globalised media, those cases could spread the reputational damage from the individual firm to Australia itself.

Politics abhors a vacuum, and if our leaders won't talk up the temporary work visa program, others will talk it down. The risk is a self-fulfilling cycle of insularity. We continue to run a mass-migration program, but as an entitled host, berating the new arrival to sign up to our values or face demonisation. Here, politics is actively undermining the national interest. Parochialism doesn't persuade skilled migrants to become Australian. On the contrary, it encourages them to see Australia as a posting, not a home. It allows Canada or New Zealand to steal our crown as the world's greatest migrant nation. And it emboldens Beijing in its attempt to monitor the Chinese in Australia. We can only counter that influence with an active strategy of engagement. In other words, play the loyalty game on our terms, as a welcoming host.

This will require a new approach to integration. In the past, it took two generations to count the success of a migration wave. The new arrival started at the bottom. It was the second generation, their Australian-born children, who rose to positions of authority in parliament, the public service, media and business.

We cannot afford to wait a generation with the Chinese or, indeed, the Indians. Their success on arrival has to be reflected more quickly in our institutions. I am not suggesting that we hand over political or corporate power to the skilled migrant, but that we learn to share it. The alternative is a withdrawn migrant elite who lives in comfortable separation from the rest of the population.

Every migrant is a potential emissary. Welcome them, and their mother country will view Australia more favourably. Alienate them, and their mother country will be less inclined to do us a favour. This is a risk I suspect our politicians do not appreciate. How will China and India treat us in international forums in the future if we refuse to engage with their sons and daughters who want to live here?

Australia's place in the twenty-first century will turn on this basic question of identity. Will we be comfortable in our Eurasian skin? If the answer is yes, then our old Anglo and European allies, and our rising neighbours in the region, will have a mutual interest in our prosperity. We will never be big enough to force the world to listen to us. But we can inspire it by our example.

Towards independence

John Howard often said that our engagement with Asia should be on proudly Australian terms: that is, we didn't have to assimilate to be accepted in the region. Depending on the audience, that message was taken as a soft form of xenophobia or as a surprising declaration of Eurasian neutrality, secure in our Anglo heritage and confident in our Asian future.

The first iteration of that argument, made when Howard was Opposition leader in the mid-1990s, had a plainly domestic political purpose. He wanted to paint Paul Keating's push for a republic and greater engagement with Asia as un-Australian. This is how he put the argument in his "headland" speech on national identity in 1995: "I don't believe that Australia faces some kind of exclusive choice between our past and our future, between our history and our geography. To me such a choice is phoney and irrelevant – only posed by those with ulterior motives."

But tweak that argument for an international audience and the meaning shifts in an unexpected way. Consider this exchange at a press conference at the United Nations in May 2003. Asked if Australia's involvement in Iraq reflected a split between the Anglo-Saxon bloc and Europe, which wanted no part in the war, Howard replied with a bet each way:

Australia in a way occupies quite a unique intersection of culture, history and geography. We are a nation of western European roots. We have a very strong linkage and association with the United States, but we also have very important linkages with and a very important future invested in ... the countries of our region. So I am not into putting Australia into particular spheres – Anglo or otherwise – nor am I into making a choice.

In one respect, it was a strange answer. Howard had in fact made a controversial choice – to join George W. Bush's coalition of the willing. (Remember that the two nations closest to Australia in terms of history, culture and ethnic mix – Canada and New Zealand – had stayed out of Iraq.) But Howard had nonetheless given voice, however unconsciously, to the ideal of an independent foreign policy. The notion that Australia should not have to choose between West and East placed him closer to the Eurasian dream of Whitlam and Keating than the Anglo deference of Menzies and Holt.

What Howard could not have realised was that his migration program would make the argument for an independent foreign policy more compelling, as Australia completes the transition from an Anglo-European to Eurasian nation. ■

MUGGED BY SENTIMENT

Revamping the US
alliance and surviving the
forty-fifth president

James Curran

Donald Trump's election as American president has led to political havoc in Washington and exposed deep social rifts across the United States – but it has also fostered divisions far from the Capitol. In Australia, the emergence of this rash and unpredictable president has highlighted stark differences in attitudes towards the 66-year-old alliance with the United States. For every voice contending that Australia should distance itself from an unpredictable White House, there has been another encouraging proactive engagement with the Trump camp. As a result, debate over the alliance has moved to the centre of Australian political life in a way not seen since the Iraq War.

The responses to Trump have broadly settled into three competing camps. The first, flowing largely from a hostility to Trump's persona – and in some cases from deep-seated cultural antipathy towards America – is an impatience for Australia to finally throw off its supposed reliance on the United States and grasp the holy grail of an "independent" foreign policy. A second camp – resorting to pragmatism – argues that the government should actively engage the new administration but lower its expectations of what can be achieved during Trump's term of office. The final response – and the one that is the most pervasive among the highest levels of the Australian government – is sentimentalism, a reliance on the history of the alliance as a means of shoring up the relationship against chill Trumpian headwinds. The sentimentalists, who also include an influential section of the commentariat, look to the future by looking back – and they are convinced that this will reinforce the nation's reliability as a close US ally.

Understanding the claims of these camps is crucial if the country is to come to grips with what a strikingly different America means for Australia's future in Asia. It will certainly mean keeping a close watch on how the forces roiling US politics are affecting America's self-belief, and thus the course of its foreign policy. But it will also mean that the ascendancy of the sentimentalist camp during the past twenty years will look increasingly shaky, and that Australia will have to recast its approach to the alliance. The question that policymakers will need to face – even if they wish they did not have to – is whether the US can continue to provide the global and regional leadership that underpins Australia's deep attachment to the alliance relationship.

The post-Trump malaise

Trump's elevation to the presidency has caused much anxiety about the future of the alliance. Fearful that the new president's lurid campaign prescriptions for the virtual trashing of the US alliance system in Asia might become reality, some analysts understandably saw only the darkest of clouds gathering as Trump came to office.

A more alarmist version of this response harked back to much older fears that have periodically haunted the Australian strategic imagination: namely, that a great power protector was about to abandon the nation altogether. Thus, the head of the Australian Strategic Policy Institute, Peter Jennings, said that if Trump's vision for the US alliance system in Asia was enacted, "you'd have that sense of US disengagement – not going any further west than Hawaii." Such comments carried more than a whiff of the panic that gripped Australian policymakers in 1969, when President Richard Nixon, in light of a deteriorating situation on the ground in Vietnam, pledged that the US would never again involve itself in a land war in Asia. He wanted US allies to provide more for their own self-defence. Australia's then Secretary of the Department of Foreign Affairs, Keith Waller, reached the sombre conclusion at the time that the "US retreat from Asia" meant a "major withdrawal from the whole area west of Hawaii." At a time when the anxiety prompted by the very words "east of Suez" prompted feverish reactions to the United Kingdom's earlier announcement of its planned military withdrawal from South-East Asia, the same eerie resonance was clearly being deployed in Waller's – and Jennings' – language.

This view only seemed to gain strength in the wake of that first, tense telephone exchange between the president and the Australian prime minister in January 2017, when Trump angrily questioned Turnbull about why he should have to honour a refugee resettlement deal agreed to by President Obama. When Trump fulminated that it was the "worst call by far" that day – this, only hours after he had spoken with Russian president Vladimir Putin – it seemed to confirm that the alliance was headed for turbulence.

The gloom deepened as chaos and dysfunction not only engulfed Trump's early days in office but seemed to become something of a modus operandi for a White House permanently under siege and at war with Republicans on Capitol Hill, the judiciary and much of the American media. Trump's decision to withdraw the US from the Trans-Pacific Partnership (TPP) and the Paris Agreement on climate change, his impatience with international summitry and his flippancy with the use of classified intelligence all seemed to reinforce a sense that "America First" really translated into "America Alone." Sighs of relief were heard when the president ordered air strikes on Syria, refrained from following through on some of his more punitive economic policies towards China, and signalled more American troops for Afghanistan. But many of Trump's prescriptions and his early performances as president have only served to bolster the disdain felt towards him.

The sentimentalists of Canberra

Despite widespread concerns about the Trump administration, the response that has predominated in terms of both alliance pomp and, in some respects, Australian policy is sentimentalism. It is characterised either by a determination to make the new, uncertain times fit the established pattern, or by a reversion to wilful nostalgia. Here, the tendency is either to bask in the cosy glow of recycled rhetoric, or to line up even more forcefully and absolutely behind American policy. Thus, Malcolm Turnbull felt the need to affirm in the wake of Trump's election win that "Americans understand that they have no stronger ally, no better friend, than Australia." And at the end of his January conversation with the president, he told Trump that "you can count on me. I will be there again and again," a pledge the prime minister honoured when, in the midst of feverish war talk over North Korean nuclear belligerence, he remarked that the two countries were "joined at the hip" and promised to invoke the ANZUS Treaty in the event of a direct attack on the United States by Pyongyang. The proviso was significant – there can be little doubt that an Australian government of either political colour would invoke ANZUS in the event of such a clear-cut case of military aggression against the United States – but the commitment only seemed to validate the president's hot-headedness and invite the charge that Turnbull had given the administration a blank cheque of Australian support. Far wiser to follow established precedent and keep these kinds of assurances private.

Only the crazy-brave would advocate the government coming out and publicly criticising the White House – in the early 1970s Gough Whitlam found that such an approach only had deleterious effects on

Australian access and influence in Washington – but what has been noticeable is the steadfast refusal on the part of senior ministers to even acknowledge a changing American mood. Thus, Foreign Minister Julie Bishop, speaking in Los Angeles in January, praised the "corresponding worldview" that the two countries shared – this despite Trump's determination, and subsequent decision, to withdraw from the TPP. And at the Shangri-La Dialogue on security in Singapore, Defence Minister Marise Payne told reporters that she didn't even need to listen to Secretary of Defence James Mattis's speech to gain reassurance of "the attitude and engagement of the United States in the region." At a time when there is widespread doubt and disillusion in the Asia-Pacific as to the shape of the new administration's Asia policy, the comments are indicative of a certain complacency within the Turnbull ministry.

The sentimental view is supported by those organisations that tend towards a dewy-eyed perspective on the alliance, such as the American Australian Association, formed in 1948 by Sir Keith Murdoch to build on the links forged in wartime, and the Australian American Leadership Dialogue, a private initiative established by businessman Phil Scanlan, which convenes an annual gathering of policymakers and commentators from both sides of the Pacific. Some attendees of the dialogue now privately concede that it is approaching obsolescence, given the lack of serious American political heft it attracts. However, the most visible demonstration of the reliance on sentimentalism came in May, aboard the USS *Intrepid* in New York, when Trump and Turnbull commemorated the seventy-fifth anniversary of the Battle of the Coral Sea. Seen as a chance for reconciliation for the two leaders after the brusque exchange over the phone at the beginning of the year, the event represented the high point of the fusion between the alliance and the Anzac legend, a phenomenon that first began in earnest during the prime ministership of John Howard. Aboard a floating museum docked off Manhattan, dinner guests were shown stirring videos drawing a line all the way from Australians and Americans fighting at Le Hamel in 1918 to the contemporary conflicts in the Middle East. From that swelling reverie emerged consensus among many in the press that these kinds of rituals were now an indelible characteristic of the relationship, and, moreover, that

> **Only the crazy-brave would advocate the government publicly criticising the White House**

an enthusiastic Trump had been willingly inducted into the "sacred" rites of the alliance. All, then, it seemed, was well. A transactional president had been shown what allies could achieve together when the existential threat appeared. The moment he stepped back on shore, so this narrative ran, Trump the alliance sceptic had undergone a metamorphosis and become an alliance true believer.

The Australian government clearly believes that cuddling up to Trump offers some kind of strategic reassurance in an era of volatility. Why? Canberra's approach is not new. Over the last two decades, there has been increasing sentimentality in the US–Australia relationship.

At face value, of course, this is no bad thing. Allies will necessarily tend the flame of historical memory and – in moments of flux – history and a sense of the past offer surer ground on which to tread. The problem is that the reminiscence is tending to overwhelm the reexamination of basic assumptions about the nature of US power, and how this will affect Australian foreign and defence policy.

But there are a number of other explanations for why sentimentalism has been so dominant. One might be the desire of senior bureaucrats in the national security community to preserve it from the whims of individual leaders. That view might well be tailor-made for this Trumpian moment: the thinking here being that the best way to handle the president's unpredictability and inexperience on the world stage is to smother him in history, leaving the issues of substance to the senior policy professionals. Seen in that light, the events aboard the *Intrepid* might be understood as an adroit movement of the red cape in front of the American bull.

Another crucial dimension fuelling this emotional rendition of the relationship is the legacy of the Iraq War. Among those who supported the US invasion in 2003 – particularly in the bureaucracy and the commentariat – there is an ongoing need to extract something meaningful, something serviceable, from this disaster. Still in denial, they emphasise that Canberra achieved deeper US–Australian military integration, a free trade agreement and stronger intelligence links. But given the international environment over the last decade, there is every reason to think that the alliance would have developed this way irrespective of whether Australia had sent troops to the Middle East. The colossal failure in Iraq remains the spectre at the feast of alliance sentimentalism, inhibiting new thinking about the relationship with the US.

A more likely driver of this sentimentalism is the collision of two powerful forces: the anxiety resulting from China's rise, and a lack of clarity about how the new American administration perceives Asia. Canberra clearly believes that by appealing to America's historical role in the region, it can somehow help to arrest isolationist trends in Washington. By doing so, it simply assumes that the United States will continue to play the same regional role it has since the end of World War II.

While Australia – along with every other regional US ally – continues to resist American pressure to join the US in freedom of navigation patrols through the contested twelve-nautical-mile zone, elsewhere Australian policy towards China is hardening. In March 2017, the foreign minister took the unprecedented step of stating publicly that Beijing would never reach its full potential unless it embraced democracy. No previous Australian foreign minister or prime minister had taken this position. During a major speech in Singapore, Turnbull laid down some sharp lines of his own, stating that a "coercive China would find its neighbours resenting demands they cede their autonomy and strategic space, and look to counter-weight Beijing's power by bolstering alliances and partnerships, between themselves and especially with the United States." And he continued to point to Asia's success as one based on the "freedom of the rules-based framework, the Pax Americana."

Waking up to the new America

Turnbull's sentimental appeal to the Pax Americana – still the fall-back position in Canberra – reveals a great deal about how Australia is faring in understanding the forces moving beneath the surface of political events in the United States. It shows the deep roots of Australian faith in the role of global leadership that the US has performed since the 1940s, and a reluctance to let go of that American vision. Put starkly, as the exceptionalist faith is being invoked here it continues to face real pressures in the United States: most particularly a deep sense of fatigue in the American heartland with the human and financial costs expended in the name of "democracy promotion," especially in the Middle East. Trump's crude style and crass behaviour and his longstanding criticism of alliances and multilateralism have unsurprisingly become the lightning rod for claims that America's special providence is being abruptly and cursorily undermined. But the roots of this current American malaise are not to be found in Trump's election alone. He is in many respects the product of an era, stretching back to 9/11, in which American prestige, credibility and ability to influence global events have been steadily dissipating.

The fate of American exceptionalism is now an urgent question for Australia, as it is for other close US allies. Greater energy needs to be devoted to understanding the current American dilemma: namely,

Never again miss an issue. Subscribe and save.

☐ **1 year auto-renewing print and digital subscription** (3 issues) $49.99 incl. GST (save 29%).

☐ **1 year print and digital subscription** (3 issues) $59.99 incl. GST (save 15%).

☐ **2 year print and digital subscription** (6 issues) $114.99 incl. GST (save 20%).

☐ Tick here to commence subscription with the current issue.

ALL PRICES INCLUDE POSTAGE AND HANDLING.

PAYMENT DETAILS I enclose a cheque/money order made out to Schwartz Publishing Pty Ltd.
Or please debit my credit card (MasterCard, Visa or Amex accepted).

CARD NO. ☐☐☐☐ ☐☐☐☐ ☐☐☐☐ ☐☐☐☐

EXPIRY DATE ____ / ____   CCV _____   AMOUNT $ _____

CARDHOLDER'S NAME _____

SIGNATURE _____

NAME _____

ADDRESS _____

_____

EMAIL _____   PHONE _____

Freecall: 1800 077 514 **or** +61 3 9486 0288 **email:** subscribe@australianforeignaffairs.com **australianforeignaffairs.com**
Digital-only subscriptions are available from our website: australianforeignaffairs.com/subscribe

An inspired gift. Subscribe a friend.

☐ **1 year print and digital subscription** (3 issues) $59.99 incl. GST (save 15%).

☐ **2 year print and digital subscription** (6 issues) $114.99 incl. GST (save 20%).

☐ Tick here to commence subscription with the current issue.

ALL PRICES INCLUDE POSTAGE AND HANDLING.

PAYMENT DETAILS I enclose a cheque/money order made out to Schwartz Publishing Pty Ltd.
Or please debit my credit card (MasterCard, Visa or Amex accepted).

CARD NO. ☐☐☐☐ ☐☐☐☐ ☐☐☐☐ ☐☐☐☐

EXPIRY DATE ____ / ____   CCV _____   AMOUNT $ _____

CARDHOLDER'S NAME _____   SIGNATURE _____

NAME _____

ADDRESS _____

EMAIL _____   PHONE _____

RECIPIENT'S NAME _____

RECIPIENT'S ADDRESS _____

RECIPIENT'S EMAIL _____   PHONE _____

Freecall: 1800 077 514 **or** +61 3 9486 0288 **email:** subscribe@australianforeignaffairs.com **australianforeignaffairs.com**
Digital-only subscriptions are available from our website: australianforeignaffairs.com/gift

Delivery Address:
LEVEL 1, 221 DRUMMOND ST
CARLTON VIC 3053

Australian Foreign Affairs
REPLY PAID 90094
CARLTON VIC 3053

No stamp required
if posted in Australia

Delivery Address:
LEVEL 1, 221 DRUMMOND ST
CARLTON VIC 3053

Australian Foreign Affairs
REPLY PAID 90094
CARLTON VIC 3053

the effort to reconcile its deepest beliefs about its national image and purpose with its increasingly limited capacity to effect transformational change abroad. In short, the United States is still too powerful to possess the humility to share the load of global leadership, but not powerful enough to demand obeisance from allies regardless of the circumstances. This complex balancing act is tailor-made for misunderstanding on both sides, and it is made all the more complex and fraught by Trump's style of governing.

Turnbull's continued faith in the Pax Americana is hardly surprising: all Australian prime ministers have in one sense or another harnessed their views of the alliance to the rock of postwar American global leadership and the regional stability it has provided for the Asia-Pacific. But it has been the very absence of Trump's appeal to the Pax Americana that has so unnerved US allies in Europe and Asia. Neither in his campaign speeches nor in his inaugural address did Trump invoke this national myth of the United States having a preordained mission to redeem the world. Trump continued to eschew this kind of role for the US when, in his first address to a joint session of Congress, he maintained that it was not his job to "represent the world." Even in committing more troops to Afghanistan, he was quick to stress that it was not with "nation-building" in mind. Tempting though it might be to assert that this renewed commitment to a forward presence for American troops abroad, along with his strike on Syria and his belated honouring of the collective defence clause in the NATO treaty, constitute a resumption of "normal programming" – or the reassertion of the Washington diplomatic elite, or "blob," as it is now referred to pejoratively – it remains too early to tell whether Trump will fully embrace a more traditional US outlook. In announcing his Afghanistan strategy, he made sure to express his shared "frustration" with the American people "over a foreign policy that has spent too much time, energy, money – and most importantly lives – trying to rebuild countries in our own image instead of pursuing our security interests above all other considerations."

But how deep runs this popular suspicion of American globalism? Is this nothing more than a passing phase, a recrudescence of previous periods of self-doubt and introspection in the United States? While the angry, divisive and populist tenor in American political debate has found its strongest expression in the nativist sentiment that backed Trump to the Republican nomination and the presidency, it also helped fuel Bernie Sanders' candidacy in the Democratic Party. It was present, too, in Hillary Clinton's abandonment of the TPP and her more sceptical attitude to free trade. It also found expression, if for much less populist reasons, in President Obama's resetting of US foreign policy. Obama argued that while America still largely sets the international agenda, it "can't fix everything." Where the advancement of US security interests and values is concerned, America would have to "pick and choose our spots" and "recognise that there are going to be times where the best that we can do is to shine a spotlight on something that's terrible, but not believe that we can automatically solve it."

Few in Canberra in recent years have stopped to question what a world without this kind of American pre-eminence would look like, though Tony Abbott, when Opposition leader, revealed the underlying unease at such a prospect during a speech in Washington in 2012. Abbott confessed that "none of us should want to find out the hard way what a shrunken America might mean," adding further that "America is exceptional so exceptionalism has its place." It needs to be remembered that the worldview of the current generation of Australian leaders was shaped primarily in the era of the Cold War. They are not used to an America on the back foot, an America not prepared to lead at every turn. Australian leaders talk publicly of the model of US global leadership they want, rather than the America they are faced with: one buffeted by gusty isolationist and protectionist headwinds.

The roots of this current American malaise are not to be found in Trump's election alone

The new president may be accelerating the trend of relative US decline, and questioning key pillars of the liberal international order, but American "credibility" on the world stage suffered substantial damage during the presidencies of his two predecessors. As foreign affairs analyst Tom Switzer has pointed out, feverish post–Cold War talk of the US as the "indispensable nation," or visions of "benign liberal hegemony," all "changed when America squandered its blood and treasure in needless wars and suffered its greatest financial crisis since the Great Depression." Any talk of Trump's undermining of the postwar order cannot simply ignore the damage done to US prestige by the 2003 invasion of Iraq, abuses at Abu Ghraib prison, and Obama's blunders in Libya and Syria.

Little wonder, then, that there is a great deal of soul-searching, if not profound anxiety, among some political elites in the US about the ideological foundation of American power. Henry Kissinger makes the point that Americans have become "too indulgent in challenging what used to be core national beliefs." As Kissinger puts it, while "the notion of American exceptionalism still exists," the idea of the country as a "shining city on a hill" is weakening. Kissinger expressed the view that the American public could still be convinced of this higher calling for the US in the world, but that they would require a different explanation from the one that was valid in the 1950s. Kissinger is not alone. Council on Foreign Relations president Richard Haass, former deputy secretary of state Robert Zoellick and prominent *Washington Post* columnist Richard Cohen, among others, have also called for the rediscovery of America's global mission.

So far, Trump has shown no inclination to take on this task. What, in any case, are the grounds for believing that future presidential candidates will move to restore this kind of vision? There is every reason to suspect that Trump's critique of the missionary impulse in US foreign policy may gain stronger purchase in American politics in future.

The nationalists and the pragmatists

The sentimentalist approach has been joined by two other main responses to the Trump administration. One, inspired by deep streams of Australian cultural nationalism, believes that Trump offers yet another opportunity for Canberra to break free of what they see as an American straitjacket. The other finds reassurance in a reading of the alliance which recognises that from time to time it has been a relationship characterised by unfulfilled expectations on both sides.

At one end were the remarks of former prime minister Paul Keating, who called on Canberra to "cut the tag" with the United States and finally embrace a more "independent" Australian foreign policy, especially in Asia. Keating was by no means talking about the abrogation of ANZUS – while attacking the "sacramental" quality afforded it by both sides of politics, he still welcomed the benefits accruing to Australia from the alliance. But his description of Australia "tagging along" behind the US still derived largely from a "radical nationalist" view of the nation's past, which claims that the country has never been able to lay claim to a separate international identity and has only been a "lickspittle" to the interests of great and powerful friends like Britain and the United States.

At other times, and in line with the approach taken by the Whitlam and Hawke governments, and indeed his own, Keating has stressed the need for Australia to express greater "self-reliance" within and sometimes without the alliance. The emphasis on "self-reliance" is much more useful than the seemingly ritual clarion calls – mostly from former diplomats – for greater Australian "independence" in the conduct of its foreign policy. Such calls rest on an equally flawed interpretation of Australian history and tend to depict the nation's past as a saga of unending servility to London and Washington. But since the late nineteenth century, colonial and then Commonwealth leaders have not only perceived distinct national interests in Asia, they have never hesitated to express their frustration and disagreement with leaders in both Britain and the United States who fail to understand Australia's search for security in the Pacific.

The more extreme view of this radical nationalist position is to be found in the stance of Greens leader Richard Di Natale, who argued that the alliance under Trump now represents "a security threat to Australia." Echoing the late Malcolm Fraser, Di Natale pronounced Washington a "dangerous ally" and more recently has called for the "ditching" of the alliance altogether. Independent senator Nick Xenophon, citing a growing gulf in the notion of Australia's shared values with a United States under Trump's leadership, has called for a "rethink" of the alliance.

As with similar calls in the past for the virtual abandonment of the ANZUS Treaty, there is rarely a credible argument put forward for how Australia would pay for the costs of its own national defence without the US alliance, nor is there a weighing up of the consequences of the loss to Australia's intelligence capabilities, the benefits that flow in terms of access to US defence materiel, and, crucially, the basic deterrent that the ANZUS Treaty provides for Australia.

Both the radical nationalist and the alarmist positions have tended to see the Trump phenomenon in isolation, forgetting that the alliance in the past has had to weather not only the vicissitudes of presidential personality, but also swift shifts in American policy at other times of geopolitical change. Richard Nixon's presidency, for example, saw widespread unease in Canberra over the nature of America's commitment to Asia, and ultimately generated such heated disagreement that consideration was given in Washington to ending the alliance with Australia altogether. Differences over trade, the shape of Asian regional architecture and especially policy towards Indonesia punctuated the relationship throughout the 1980s and '90s. But the alliance has been able to withstand periodic crises and endured under governments of both persuasions.

Accordingly, the pragmatic realist response to the new president is primarily concerned with how to manage Trump so as to preserve the alliance from his unpredictability and volatility. It concedes that anything resembling a coherent Trump doctrine is unlikely to emerge. Here, the mantra has been to simply take Trump one step at a time, engage other levels of the administration below the presidency, keep faith with the deepening integration of the respective military establishments and assume that churn in US policy will be the norm for the foreseeable future.

Two of Australia's most respected foreign and defence policy mandarins have given the most coherent expression to this view. The former head of foreign affairs, Peter Varghese, has stated that the alliance will survive "whatever dramas the Trump administration brings," stressing the need for Australia to ride out the period but recognise that "our expectations of each other are going to be quite low." Similarly, the recently retired defence department secretary and former Australian ambassador to Washington Dennis Richardson, has cautioned against allowing the "poison evident in US domestic politics to infect our attitudes to the alliance." Any debate and reassessment of the value of the alliance, he adds, "should flow from clear eyed analysis and judgment, not the emotional reaction to one person." The argument here is about continuity, but continuity with a measure of caution and reserve. Neither Richardson nor Varghese is under any illusion that the forces which brought Trump to power represent a substantial challenge to how Australia navigates an increasingly complex international environment.

How to survive forty-five

For all the sense of shock and outrage at the challenge thrown down by Trump to many of the established conventions of diplomacy, it also has to be recognised that his presidency so far has not resulted in the widespread collapse of the US alliance system – in either Europe or Asia – or indeed the dissolution of the liberal international order. Trump has put both systems under severe strain, to be sure – but it is likely that Sanders or Clinton would have followed the same Trumpian path in certain respects, especially on some trade matters. In much the same way that the press, Congress and the judiciary have checked and balanced his domestic agenda, so too have international circumstances and the office of the presidency moderated some of his wilder tendencies. The Iranian nuclear deal remains in place, and it was notable that in his remarks to justify the increase in American troops for Afghanistan, Trump publicly backed away from his "original instinct ... to pull out" and opted instead to follow the advice of his military advisers. The decision itself is unlikely to change much on the ground in what remains an unwinnable war, but it may come to stand as a revealing moment in the Trump presidency. The question for this US president has always been whether he had the capacity to change once he assumed the office – whether his strong impulses would be mugged by reality.

Elsewhere, Japan and South Korea have not been harassed to stump up for the costs of paying for the cost of housing and feeding US troops, and US–China relations, though strained over Trump's unrealistic expectation of Beijing's capacity to bring about change in North Korean behaviour, remain steady, if occasionally tense. The threats to label China a currency manipulator or slap a 45 per cent tariff on Chinese imports have not come to pass, and feverish White House talk of a "trade war" has cooled – though by no means evaporated – with Steve Bannon's departure from the administration.

Still, the idea that the passing of Trump from the scene will remove the toxicity from American politics is surely a fantasy. And it is not entirely out of the question that he can still do great damage to both key American relationships and the international system. North

Korean nuclear belligerence remains the only serious crisis Trump has thus far faced, and his response typified the very kind of impetuous and impulsive style that so unnerves close US allies. At the moment of South Korea's greatest vulnerability, he accused its government of "appeasement" and threatened to terminate the Korea–US trade deal. Too much optimism, it seems, is being placed in the restraining capabilities of the troika of "adults" in the administration: Secretary of State Rex Tillerson, Secretary of Defence James Mattis and National Security Adviser H.R. McMaster. Trump's moments of presidential gravitas are but fleeting glimpses before the next self-inflicted drama diverts the White House from its agenda.

The alliance with the US has proved its resilience before and it will survive Trump. Nevertheless, the past offers both reassuring and troubling insights into how the Australian policy and political community deals with profound shocks to its view of the world. It is salutary to recall that the most seismic change in Australia's international outlook in the twentieth century, the collapse of British race patriotism, came largely in response to steps taken not in Canberra but in London. It took well over thirty years to wrench the British imperial ideal clean from the Australian strategic imagination, the conviction that Australian and British interests ought ultimately to coincide. Faith in Empire defence – the belief that Britain would come to assist Australia in its hour of crisis – even outlasted the Fall of Singapore in 1942, and only after the momentous decisions of successive British governments to pursue an economic future in Europe and pull out their military from South-East

Asia did Australian politicians start setting new coordinates for their foreign and defence policy. Only then did they start to conceive of a world without Britain. That process began around the same time that Australia was giving its alliance with the United States new meaning by freely committing to the cause in Vietnam, but it ultimately ended in both political sides reaching a consensus on the need to prioritise "comprehensive engagement" with Asia.

Still, all of this took place against the backdrop of US regional primacy. China is now challenging America's regional influence like never before. It is some time now since defence analyst Hugh White made the telling point that "primacy is the only form of strategic engagement true to America's exceptional nature." In other words, the most powerful currents of American nationalism simply cannot conceive of China as an equal, much less cede credibility to the notion of a coming Chinese pre-eminence. This is a painful and deeply disturbing process for a country built on a powerful national myth about its global reach and redemptive mission. There is every reason, then, for the Australian government to do some harder thinking about what this different America means for Australia and Asia.

We are not at the point of being able to discern a sure or consistent pattern of American retreat from Asia. But the overall picture is complex. Washington's allies in Asia neither follow the US through the contested waters of the South China Sea, nor take a hardline stance against Beijing in the councils of ASEAN. Indeed, they continue to engage Beijing pragmatically. Still, these same allies do not clamour for the United States to pack up and leave. But jostling against the frequent protestations of American regional staying power are the nagging doubts created by various recalibrations of US Asia policy since the late 1960s: the Nixon Doctrine, the eventual abandonment of South Vietnam, the "shock" of the American opening to China, and the cutting of official ties to Taiwan. Australia has to at least start thinking what the possible consequences might be for the alliance in Asia if the angry, inward-looking mood in the United States solidifies over the medium to long term.

Sentimentalism in the alliance can occasionally serve the moment well, and it has the benefit of connecting the present with the past. But it can never be a standalone strategy for managing the relationship. Rather, it can fuel an expectation in Washington that Australia will always be there. The argument that such a stance guarantees Australia access and influence is only partially right. History shows that it can also relegate the nation to the status of an ally whose support is simply taken for granted. For the time being, then, taking Trump one step at a time remains the best option for Australia. Engage, yes, but do so with prudence. For this is a White House and a president that lurches from one crisis to the next, and Australia cannot afford to be hit by falling debris. ■

CAN KIM JONG-UN BE STOPPED?

A report on the
North Korean
missile crisis

John Delury

The Supreme Leader

The year in North Korea always begins with the Supreme Leader. Kim Jong-un stands at a wooden lectern, flanked by the emblem of the Workers' Party of Korea, which symbolises unity between workers (a hammer), farmers (a sickle) and intellectuals (a brush). He sings the praises of revolutionary accomplishment for the year just ended and lays out priorities for the year ahead. Television sets across the country will run the New Year's address on loop, so that no one can miss the Respected Leader's message, although the content is fairly predictable. This year, however, Kim ended with a startling confession:

> As I am standing here to proclaim the beginning of another year,
> I feel a surge of anxiety about what I should do to hold our people

in greater reverence . . . My desires were burning all the time, but I spent the past year feeling anxious and remorseful for the lack of my ability. I am hardening my resolve to seek more tasks for the sake of the people this year and make redoubled, devoted efforts to this end.

It was a revealing moment in which Kim showed his populist sentimentalism, his willingness to admit shortcomings and his drive for success.

But Kim's lament received scant attention outside North Korea. Instead, the world heard just one single sentence from the long speech, the one in which Kim noted that his military "entered the final stage of preparation for the test launch of [an] intercontinental ballistic missile." US President-elect Donald Trump fired back a tweet. "North Korea just stated that it is in the final stages of developing a nuclear weapon capable of reaching parts of the U.S. It won't happen!" Trump declared, with his trademark exclamation point. The stage was set for a year of crisis that would keep North Korea near or at the top of Trump's foreign policy agenda.

The crisis has captivated the world's attention, but much of the coverage and analysis has focused on the latest provocation: gleeful post-test images from Pyongyang, wrathful tweets from Washington, and speculation on what each side would do next. These elements, alone, are insufficient for understanding this crisis or developing a response. In looking back on the twists and turns of the yearlong

North Korea crisis, which spiked first in April and then again in August, we can identify the deeper factors that prevent the United States and its allies – including Australia – from making any progress on the North Korean nuclear issue. When we take a closer look at the underlying causes of the ongoing crisis, a clearer picture emerges of the extent of the risk of a nuclear tragedy, and of the blind spot that has been preventing Washington from taking the necessary action to try to avert it.

The Ides of April

After that New Year's sparring between Kim and Trump, things stayed quiet for just over a month. Pyongyang had not tested any missiles since the previous October, and as Trump's National Security Council began a North Korea policy review, there was a sense that this highly unconventional president might actually go through with his campaign talk of a "hamburger summit" with the young North Korean leader. A senior North Korean diplomat was due to visit New York in late February for an unofficial "track two" meeting, to be held just a half-dozen blocks from Trump Tower – a convenient excuse to jump-start backchannel dialogue.

But hopes of getting off on the right foot were tripped up when Kim Jong-un abruptly ended the de facto missile test moratorium on 11 February. More spectacularly, two days later, Kim's elder half-brother Kim Jong-nam was assassinated at Kuala Lumpur airport in a covert operation that was as cunning as it was cruel. Malaysian authorities announced that the murder weapon had been VX, a highly toxic nerve agent, administered by young women from Vietnam and Indonesia, who claimed to have thought they were part of a harmless prank. The track two meeting in Manhattan was called off, and some of Trump's advisers may have reached dire conclusions about the brutality of their adversary in Pyongyang.

Tensions mounted throughout the early spring, as North Korea tested missile after missile, and the United States and Republic of Korea (ROK) staged two months of large-scale joint military exercises. The North Korea policy review was hurried to a conclusion in advance of Trump's Mar-a-Lago summit with Chinese president Xi Jinping, reflecting the central role that Beijing played in the administration's calculus. The shorthand for the new policy was "maximum pressure and engagement" – meaning engage China to put maximum pressure on North Korea. Trump even vowed to go easy on trade disputes with China, so long as President Xi helped him put pressure on Kim. But Trump also warned darkly that if Beijing let him down, he would turn to military options in order to solve the North Korea problem alone – with force and without warning.

Trump's allusions to letting slip the dogs of war brought the sense of crisis to a boiling point by mid-April, when it was feared that North Korea would celebrate a major national holiday with an intercontinental ballistic missile (ICBM) test. But instead, at the parade in Kim Il-sung Square to celebrate the national founder's birth on 15 April 1912, his grandson Kim Jong-un merely showed off a new *intermediate*-range ballistic missile, which failed in flight during its tests that month. Spring on the Korean Peninsula came in like a lion but went out like a lamb.

The guns of August

As the crisis with North Korea seemed to abate, Americans became preoccupied by Russiagate, and the drama of the FBI director's firing and testimony before Congress. But Kim's rocket experts were hard at work. They "redoubled devoted efforts," staging four more missile tests that included a successful launch of the new intermediate-range missile. And then, in July, it happened. North Korea successfully tested an ICBM, in what they called the "July 4 Revolution." This was followed by another successful test they called the "July 28 Great Victory." The president-elect's red line was crossed.

In response to the ICBM tests, Trump's envoy to the United Nations, Ambassador Nikki Haley, convinced China and Russia to sign off on a new round of robust sanctions. The UN Security Council measures amounted to a partial trade and investment embargo: a complete ban on exports of North Korea's major trade products (coal, iron, lead and seafood), and a freeze on new joint ventures, foreign investments and hiring of expatriate workers. But President Trump, on working vacation, was not satisfied with his 15–0 victory at the Security Council. At a press conference to discuss the nation's opioid crisis, Trump folded his arms sternly and, pretending to read from notes, warned Kim Jong-un that if North Korea did not stop threatening the United States, "They will be met with fire, fury and frankly power, the likes of which this world has never seen before."

Telling North Korea not to threaten America is like telling a kangaroo not to jump. Sure enough, Kim crossed Trump's new red line before the paint had dried. Within hours of the "fire and fury" comment, the North Korean military released statements describing a "plan" they were working on to launch missiles in the international waters around Guam, home to the B-1B Lancer strategic bombers whose flights over South Korea infuriate the North. This novel plan to "envelope" (without actually striking) Guam with a volley of four intermediate-range missiles was intended to "contain" the B-1Bs.

Just like in mid-April, tensions mounted in anticipation of the mid-August deadline when Kim was supposed to decide whether or not to move forward with the Guam plan. Trump doubled down on his "fire and fury" talk ("maybe that statement wasn't tough enough"), but his cabinet walked the rhetoric back. Secretary of State Rex Tillerson and Secretary of Defense James Mattis penned a sober op-ed in the *Wall Street Journal* that rechristened the administration's approach "strategic accountability," emphasised the preference for diplomacy and lowered the bar for dialogue with Pyongyang. The B-1B bombers seemed to be staying put. On 15 August, Kim announced he was putting the Guam plan on ice, though he added he would closely observe the behavior of the "foolish Yankees" going forward.

Another crisis on the Korean Peninsula seemed to have quietly resolved itself into a dew. The American public had moved on, anyway – the national conversation turned from talk of war in Korea to the violence on the streets of Charlottesville, Virginia, and then to the flooded streets of Houston, Texas. In South Korea, the second annual set of joint military exercises (known as Ulchi-Freedom Guardian) went ahead as planned on 21 August, but with fewer troops than the preceding year. Secretary Tillerson went out of his way to praise Kim for demonstrating "restraint" – implying it was due to the UN sanctions. President Trump told the crowd at a pep rally in Arizona that, thanks to his own tough talk, "I believe he [Kim] is starting to respect us [Trump]."

The lull did not last. Maybe Kim took these comments as taunts, as Bonnie Glaser of the Center for Strategic and International Studies feared he might at the time. Or maybe Kim expected a bold gesture from the Americans – the dispatch of a special envoy, cancellation of the exercises – and was disappointed. Or perhaps the pause in missile testing was driven by purely technical factors, rather than political calculations.

For whatever confluence of factors, Kim found himself on the morning of 29 August sitting at a makeshift desk by the runway of the Pyongyang International Airport, watching as his new intermediate-range missile shot up to the heavens and arced towards its splashdown point in the western Pacific. By flying over the northern parts of Japan along the way, the missile elicited another wave of outrage. President Trump responded with a tweet that rejected diplomacy, griping: "The U.S. has been talking to North Korea, and paying them extortion money, for 25 years. Talking is not the answer!" The B1-B bombers came back up from Guam. The following weekend, at noon Pyongyang time, Kim's scientists detonated what they claimed was a hydrogen bomb – the sixth "man-made earthquake" and significantly more powerful than the previous test, exactly one year prior.

And so it goes.

Nuclear buttons

It is tempting, in looking back at this year of crisis between North Korea and the United States, to see it all as one big act. Donald Trump and Kim Jong-un are like professional wrestlers who go round after round, with plenty of trash talk and muscle flexing and cheers and boos from the crowd, but never really come to blows.

But then we remember that these two characters are real commanders-in-chief of real armies – the most powerful in the world in terms of sheer might versus one of the most sophisticated in terms of asymmetrical threats. Either leader could go down in history as the first to order combat use of nuclear weapons since the obliteration of Hiroshima and Nagasaki in 1945. Both can be seen as highly theatrical figures who revel in antagonism, pursue high-risk/high-reward gambits, and think well of themselves as strategists. Neither man is crazy, but both are often labelled as such and may erroneously think it of one another. Their senior-most advisers are smart men and women, but they have never visited one another's countries or interacted with their respective counterparts. Neither speaks the other's language or has an intuitive sense of his profoundly different culture. Their governments have never officially recognised one another's existence and see each other as enemies – brutal totalitarians versus bullying imperialists.

In these conditions of mutual hostility and ignorance, things could go wrong, fast. But rather than taking steps to open dialogue, reduce risks, make compromises and find an off-ramp leading towards a settlement, both sides appear bent on deterring or intimidating the other, while trying to increase their leverage. For the Trump administration, this means displays of strength and threats of "military options," while pressuring China to increase sanctions such that Kim's economic position is eroded. Despite denouncing the Obama era approach of "strategic patience," Trump too is waiting – for China to solve the problem. Wise men like Henry Kissinger and Graham Allison have stoked the fantasy that by reaching "an understanding" with China over the fate of the Korean Peninsula, Trump can convince Xi to make denuclearisation happen. This vastly overestimates Chinese influence, negates North Korean agency and leads down another strategic rabbit hole.

As Trump and his advisers wait in vain for Chinese sanctions to bring Kim to his senses (if not his knees), Kim's scientists, engineers and strategists are barrelling ahead with their program of nuclear-missile development. They have technical reasons to want to keep testing nuclear devices, as Stanford University nuclear scientist Siegfried Hecker has explained, in order to ensure their warheads are light and stable enough to withstand long-distance travel and det-onate properly. They also have reason to keep up the missile testing of intercontinental, intermediate and short-range systems, using mobile launchers at locations around the country and submarine launches at sea. With each test, Kim strengthens his deterrence capa-bility against external threats, while enhancing his stature as a leader who stands up to the great powers in order to defend the territory and pride of the plucky DPRK.

These antagonistic postures entail risks on a daily basis. There are countless ways in which "local" conflicts can erupt along the demilitarised zone or the disputed maritime boundary in the West Sea [Yellow Sea], and quickly escalate to involve the United States and its allies. Yet Americans did not pay much attention on 25 August, when Kim Jong-un oversaw massive exercises staging a mock inva-sion of two ROK-held islands in the West Sea. One of these islands, Yeonpyeong-do, was the site of the last major armed conflict between the two Koreas – an artillery battle in November 2010 that resulted in casualties on both sides. At that time, the United States played a restraining role in ensuring deescalation. What if fighting broke out in the West Sea in the current climate? And how would North-East Asia's great powers, China and Russia, respond?

Redefining the conflict

This year's ongoing provocation cycle, with the underlying risk of conflict, will continue so long as the root cause of the problem is misunderstood or ignored. The reason for the North Korea crisis is not the capabilities on either side, but rather the hostile intent that comes with them. In other words, the key issue is the *political relationships* among the principal actors – North Korea, South Korea and the United States. But Trump administration officials, top military officers and the American public are focused almost exclusively on North Korea's weapons capabilities. The current preoccupation is with the prospect of an operable nuclear-tipped ICBM – something that Americans consider "intolerable" and "unimaginable." But North Korea's nuclear-missile program, like the United States' extended nuclear deterrence and joint military exercises with South Korea, issymptomatic of

In these conditions of mutual hostility and ignorance, things could go wrong, fast

an underlying disease: the hostile relationship. And the treatment requires a long-term strategy of transforming the nature of US–DPRK and inter-Korean relations. The theory of victory should be defined in terms of terminating the enemy relationship between the DPRK, the US and the ROK. A gradual process of denuclearisation can be a measure and outgrowth of that transformation, but not its precondition.

Terminating hostility is a long-term strategy that should be pursued doggedly by leadership in Washington and Seoul. It needs to start immediately by negotiating some version of the much-discussed "dual freeze" idea. The original "dual suspension" proposal actually came from the North Koreans themselves back in January 2015. Through the UN channel in New York, the DPRK offered to suspend nuclear testing in return for an American promise to suspend joint military exercises with South Korea. The Obama administration shot down the proposal out of hand, without even exploring it. Recently, the Chinese foreign ministry proposed a new version of the "dual freeze" idea, hoping Pyongyang would impose a moratorium on nuclear and missile testing in return for the United States suspending joint military exercises. Beijing further proposes that, taking advantage of the lowered tension and positive atmosphere generated by a dual freeze, denuclearisation talks can be resumed in parallel with a new track of "peace talks."

Conceptually speaking, the Chinese proposal is useful. The problem is that it's a Chinese proposal, not a North Korean one. Xi Jinping cannot speak for Kim Jong-un. We do not know what Pyongyang wants and where they are willing to compromise, beyond the general principle that the nuclear deterrent can only be put on the negotiating table if and when the United States ends its "hostile policy and nuclear threat." That is a general framework for – and invitation to – negotiation. The details can only be probed, bartered and eventually set in the process of dialogue and negotiation itself. Until senior American officials sit down across the table from their North Korean counterparts, the process cannot even begin.

A true ally

If a diplomatic process is not initiated, the situation looks likely to continue to deteriorate. If it were to reach the point of military conflict between North Korea and the United States, Australians would have much to lose. Australia sent 17,000 troops to fight in the Korean War and remains an active and engaged "sending state" to the United Nations Command, the formal military structure under which US and allied troops maintain a presence in South Korea – participating, for example – in the US–ROK joint military exercises. Prime Minister Turnbull reminded the public, "If there's an attack on the US, the ANZUS Treaty would be invoked and Australia would come to the aid of the United States, as America would come to our aid if we were attacked." Even if Trump initiated a conflict, it would be difficult militarily and agonising diplomatically to break ranks with the Americans. In other words, Australians would be swept up in a war they did not choose. Fighting in conflict started by the Americans could put severe strains on the relationship with China, which has a formal defence treaty with North Korea and adamantly opposes military options. Like China, South Korea and Japan, Australia's economy could suffer intensely from the toll of a war that Secretary Mattis anticipated as being "tragic on an unbelievable scale."

> A small-minded ally says "yes" even when he is thinking "no."

Australia should therefore do what it can, in concert with South Korea and other concerned nations, to encourage the United States and North Korea to pursue the path of dialogue, negotiation and settlement. There is a natural temptation, especially when a problem seems far away and the adversary inscrutable, to stick to the script of loyal ally. But the consequences of getting North Korea wrong are dire, and they directly impact Australia's security and economic interests. Simply declaring loyalty to Washington or echoing calls on Beijing to apply more pressure do not move us closer to progress – even when judged by the metric of America's own long-term national interest. A small-minded ally says "yes" even when he is thinking "no," whereas a true ally voices her disagreement without compromising her fidelity. Australia has a stake in Korea, but also enjoys enough distance to see the bigger picture. Canberra can resist getting sucked up into the theatrical and ideological maelstrom of the "main event" between Kim Jong-un and Donald Trump. In order to start the shift from perpetual crisis to lasting settlement, Trump and Kim will need all the help they can get. ■

9 September 2017
Seoul, South Korea

Reviews

The Retreat of Western Liberalism
Edward Luce
Atlantic Monthly Press

The *Financial Times*, based in London, owned by the Nikkei Group in Tokyo, is the most sophisticated liberal newspaper in the English-speaking world. Less assured than the bromide-addicted *Economist*, liberal capitalism's weekly encyclical for the faithful, the *FT* also avoids the Jesuitical excesses of the *Wall Street Journal*. The paper is more like the private diary of global capitalism: the most poignant and pressing anxieties of living in a market-based world are worked out daily in its pink pages. Subscribers who submit themselves to the rigor of its weekly routine are rewarded with the weekend edition, which includes a remarkably intelligent book review section and an exquisitely mindless supplement called "How to Spend It."

As the current Washington commentator and former South Asia chief, Edward Luce is one of the *Financial Times'* stalwart contributors. His new book *The Retreat of Western Liberalism* neatly collects many of the paper's favorite themes in the form of a long essay. To his credit, Luce is acutely alive to the illness at the heart of liberal capitalism today, which he diagnoses as an autoimmune disorder. There is, as everyone knows, galloping economic inequality inside Western societies, and the postwar settlements – forged under Curtin,

Fraser, Attlee and Roosevelt – that satisfied their working classes for a time are now in disrepair. In 1973 Albert Hirschman famously likened the citizens of Third World countries to drivers in a two-lane highway entering a tunnel: the right lane was willing to tolerate the advance of the left lane for a certain period after their revolutions, but their patience was limited. Now, in a way few liberal commentators besides Hirschman foresaw, this "tunnel effect" is in plain view in the West. There is a rising intolerance for inequalities of all kinds, which has expressed itself in myriad ways: ethnonationalist entrepreneurs such as Trump, Farage and Le Pen, but also astonishing popularity for openly socialist candidates such as Bernie Sanders. If Australia has not yet experienced full populist traction, there is no shortage of figures who are waiting – not so patiently – to take advantage of any tumult.

Luce knows something about what the populist backlash looks like: he has shot guns with Rodrigo Duterte in Davao, interviewed Donald Trump in the White House, and, in an earlier incarnation, written speeches for one of the leading tribunes of liberal capitalism, Larry Summers (himself an *FT* columnist). Luce places much of the blame on a class of elites – the Clintonites and "Davos men" (the congregants who flock to the Alps for the annual meeting of the World Economic Forum) – who came to believe that, armed with the panacea of rapid economic growth, the settlements with the lower middle class could be rolled up and retired. Luce does not hold high hopes that either of these elites will learn to correct their mistakes. "Davos specialises in projecting the future from a recent past that took it by surprise," he writes, in one of the book's better lines. And: "I have yet to come across a more airtight example of groupthink than Hillaryland."

The deeper value of *The Retreat of Western Liberalism* is that it dramatises the disorientation of an intelligent liberal who has looked in the mirror and found their philosophy of history wanting. Luce seems to be aware of a blind spot in his own way of seeing the world: namely, that it has always required an enemy. The advances of liberalism as an ideology were never surer than in the eighteenth and nineteenth centuries, when the absolutist regimes of Europe were the antagonists. Though, as Harvard's Daniel Ziblatt shows in his impressive new book *Conservative Parties and the Birth of Democracy*, liberals were almost always abetted by conservative parties in this work of forging compromises with the *ancien regime* to make liberal regimes possible. In the twentieth century, when liberals faced down totalitarian regimes in the Cold War, they were forced to make concessions on civil rights and labour rights in order to take the wind out of communist propaganda. Nowadays, with no foe formidable enough to challenge liberal capitalism (China's authoritarian capitalism is not enough at odds with it, and radical Islam has not yet been able to build a significant enough economic engine to make it a real alternative), liberals have become their own worst enemies. Luce has aimed his essay at liberal readers who want to regain their ground without yielding too much to the right or the left.

But while Luce offers a reasonable diagnosis of the liberal crack-up, *The Retreat of Western Liberalism* also exhibits a series of weaknesses in current liberal thought. First, he has a regrettable tendency to present common sense as something wildly counterintuitive. Luce, for instance, makes it seem like he is going out on a limb in criticising the role of digital technology in politics: "One of the bedtime stories we tell ourselves is that technology is everybody's friend." (Who tells this bedtime story anymore, besides Mark Zuckerberg?) Second, there is also a relatively sentimental line in the book that simply exhorts people to be better and do the right thing: "[I]t is character, rather than laws, which upholds a system." (What about interests? What about power?) Third, there is a tendency to reduce the ideas of thinkers to their most clichéd receptions: Francis Fukuyama was not, as Luce contends, excited about the "end of history" in 1989 – he was instead weary about the prospect of liberalism being the last ideology left standing. Karl Marx was not, as Luce contends, incapable of imagining that wealthy elites might not have much use for the nation as a vehicle for their interests.

More severely, Luce captures the conceptual confusion in today's liberalism by regaling readers with the usual laundry list of crises facing the liberal West: cyber war, nuclear proliferation, financial improprieties, new monopolies, etc. But he provides little sense of which are the greatest problems or what the priorities should be. There is a point where Luce mentions, almost offhandedly, that capitalism may be slowing down globally, but he barely pauses to consider the political implications of such a seismic possibility. Conscious that he is a journalist prone to presentism, Luce nevertheless highlights immigration as one of the main possible threats to Western states because of the way it can threaten social welfare schemes. The same Luce who is mortified by Trump is nevertheless willing to take on a lighter version of "keep them out" policies in order to deflect Trump's appeal. "Humane immigration laws should be enforced," Luce writes, "and the link between public benefits and citizens restored." Drop the pretense of "humane" and you have a campaign slogan for any number of Australian political parties defending the liberal faith in an increasingly profane world.

Thomas Meaney

Navigating the Future: An Ethnography of Change in Papua New Guinea
Monica Minnegal and Peter D. Dwyer
ANU Press

t seemed a good, even worthy, idea at the time. In the '70s, there were half a dozen resident Australian correspondents reporting from Papua New Guinea. By 2009, when I was angling for my first reporting trip to PNG, there were just two: for the ABC and for the wire service Australian Associated Press. (By 2013, the AAP bureau would also be boarded up.)

Then a senior writer for the *Age*, I had a niche enthusiasm for reporting aid and development. Indices plotting the pulse of developing nations – maternal deaths, child health, violence, disease, education, environmental degradation, women's representation, corruption – revealed PNG as a fixture at the wrong end of many tables. Much of the half a billion dollars Australia directed to PNG each year targeted these issues. Where were the stories?

What do we hear of our nearest neighbour in the mainstream media? Let's put aside Manus, given those headlines are rarely about the island, but rather about a hazy outpost of Australian politics and refugee policy. Also exclude the Kokoda Track. While they invoke connection with the Fuzzy Wuzzy Angels, Kokoda stories are predominantly *our* stories and overlook other dimensions, like the wartime executions by Australian military of local men or demands by local landowners for a bigger piece of the tourism action. A former PNG correspondent once bemoaned to me that the only yarns he could sell to his editors were of Highlands babies named Kevin Rudd, bizarre crime and what he categorised as (pardon the hardbitten vernacular) "ooga booga" stories – tales of sorcery or

cannibals. Meanwhile, much that deserves scrutiny festers invisibly: land-grabbing on a vast scale; the devastating human toll of collapsing infrastructure; bloodshed within the footprint of resources ventures.

The most consistent PNG narratives are located in the finance pages, tracking the fortunes of resources companies. Of the landscapes being prospected or the people living there, we hear not so much. Seizing on this, I tagged a pitch to research a crazily ambitious portfolio of PNG stories onto a blockbuster mining project, the $US19 billion ExxonMobil-led PNG Liquefied Natural Gas (PNG LNG), wrangling just enough editorial budget to concoct a whirlwind Highlands itinerary.

This despite having never before set foot in confounding PNG, the most linguistically diverse nation on the planet. The arrogance was gob-smacking, but the ambition honorable. News outfits worldwide were dismantling foreign bureaus as editorial coffers ran dry. The model of insights from "our man/woman in (insert far-flung dateline)," the cornerstone for comprehending our world, was dying. A "fly-in, fly-out" style of international reporting – "parachute journalism" – was filling the void. Critics in the US warned it posed a profound threat to media credibility: "Choppering into unknown locales is a recipe for sweeping conclusions, over-arching assumptions, and silly stereotypes, not to mention factual errors." But pragmatists argued that, with thoughtful preparation, valuable work could still be done, and reporting something could be better than reporting nothing.

With notebook and fine intentions, I embarked on the first of almost a dozen trips to PNG. Initially, they ran to a frantic template, lurching from village to village, hitching rides with NGOs, police, miners – this skint model relies on ethically fraught piggybacking on the logistics of others. Arriving in a dervish aboard a dusty Troopy, a tinny plane. Scooping up interviews from women in grass skirts and men adorned with cassowary bones. Touring broken hospitals and schools. Firing questions at walking wounded fleeing tribal fights or husbands, accused sorcerers, witch torturers, pastors, elders, midwives. Within

hours, I'm gone, and will spend weeks at my desk figuring out how the morsels I've hauled home fit within the researched picture.

Meanwhile, in remote country beyond the Highlands, University of Melbourne anthropologists Monica Minnegal and Peter Dwyer have been gathering up stories and observations rather more methodically. Theirs is an epic project spanning almost thirty years. They work in the lowlands of Western Province, from sites only accessible via grass airstrips which the locals trim with bushknives and, in the early years, days of footslog across swampland. They catalogue the seismic cultural aftershock of "intruding outsiders," miners mostly, but also the likes of me, and how they "infiltrate the understanding of those whom they intrude upon."

Since 1986, the couple has learnt from and lived, on and off, among Kubo and Febi people, taking ringside seats to witness an extraordinary moment. Their theatre is within the gas fields of Juha, the as yet untapped furthest reaches of the PNG LNG.

Now the largest resource extraction in the Asia-Pacific, the

PNG LNG is expected to yield $US31 billion, one-third remaining in PNG and flowing, in part, to people whose lands produce the gas. Yet despite more than 200 shiploads of gas having set sail from PNG, the distribution of benefits to communities has been acknowledged by the companies as far too slow. Analysts at the Australian National University say landowners have yet to receive any actual royalties. Anger in the active heart of the project has inflamed bloody upheaval.

The communities where Minnegal and Dwyer have embedded are on the peaceable fringes of all this. They've documented a generation growing up watching geologists, surveyors and drilling teams come and go, expecting that when – if – the gas flows, it will bring wealth. Five wells have been sunk, but remain on hold.

A new generation has begun, and locals are still waiting for "Company," which despite its elusiveness has become a "very materialized, personalized, presence," one that has changed their lives profoundly.

To claim what is theirs, they must catalogue their connection to land in ways that satisfy corporate registers. They must articulate ancient kinships. They must identify themselves in ways that square with Western rollcalls. These are people who customarily wait for children to show their character before ascribing them a name, and whose names might change over the journey of a lifetime.

"[They] were catapulted into worlds of bureaucracy, printed words and the law. They had no prior experience that might help make sense of these new worlds. Relatively few people could read. None could comprehend the language of Acts of Parliament." In 2014, no one in the village of Suabi knew what "percentage" meant.

Navigating the Future traces the "shifts in the ways people relate to the land, to each other, and to outsiders" in pursuit of a radically different future.

"Their efforts have flowed outwards to a globalized world . . . that has no sense of the efforts that people in a remote, lowland forested corner of the world contribute on its behalf. In return, the ideological persuasions of that world, the assumptions of science and the market place that give it certainty . . . have penetrated into the very being of the people."

This is a scholarly work, but also remarkably accessible, poignant and intimate. It cracks open the door to the utterly Other. Minnegal and Dwyer are affectionate and respectful, but resist romanticism. Observing with discomfort the "sense of presumed superiority" of "Company" representatives, they also document the complicity of locals manoeuvring to achieve their ends. Change is inevitable and constant. "A new world is emerging for Kubo and Febi people, a world that they themselves are building, a world in which they are emerging as new kinds of subjects."

Such critical nuances are trampled underfoot by the most well-intentioned of outsider correspondents. Without confusing the slow rigor of ethnography with the imperatives of journalism – and within remote landscapes are so many stories that deserve to find their way urgently into the world – this work challenges journalists to think about how we might gather up truer stories. The same digital revolution that hobbled roving correspondents has empowered indigenous voices to broadcast from ground zero of their realities, yet we resist hearing them. How do we enhance our storytelling by "plucking out" as opposed to parachuting in?

The powerful lesson I had learnt by the time I was making my fifth or sixth trip to PNG was how little I understood. I travelled slower. I watched. I tried to ask what I left behind when I flew away with my story, borrowing the medical principle: first, do no harm. What I have discovered from the journey with Minnegal and Dwyer is what I long suspected, but chose not to see.

Jo Chandler

Easternisation: War and Peace in the Asian Century

Gideon Rachman

Bodley Head

A Chinese friend here in Beijing was talking the other day about the difference between *xifang* and *dongfang* – the West and the East. She said that "of course" Australia, which she hasn't visited, is a country of *xifangren* – Westerners – and described their Caucasian physical features. But this stereotype can no longer be applied to Australia, with its many ethnicities, including a million citizens of Chinese heritage.

So is Australia "Western" or "Asian"? Most people would still say Western. But in many aspects, including our economy, culture and sport (Australia in 2015 not only hosted but won the Asian Cup, the premier contest in the region's premier sport, soccer), we increasingly appear more Asian.

The title of distinguished *Financial Times* journalist Gideon Rachman's book, *Easternisation*, therefore raises questions for Australians, for whom "the Orient," a region in our time zone, has never resonated as it once did in London.

But Rachman's focus is power relations: "The West's centuries-long domination of world affairs is now coming to a close. The root cause of this change is the extraordinary economic development in Asia over the last fifty years." Essentially, he means America's decline and China's rise – not a novel theme for Australian readers. It is five years since the Gillard government published the *Australia in the Asian Century* white paper, and Rachman's book references Australian academic Hugh White's *The China Choice*, also published in 2012.

But the extent to which East Asia's infrastructure, both physical and online, wildly surpasses that in North America and Europe still surprises many in Australia – where we lack almost any senior figure in politics, business, universities or the public service who has worked and lived in Asia for more than a week or two at a time.

Rachman provides a swag of quotes, anecdotes and data to support his core thesis. *Easternisation* concludes with Barack Obama's presidency fading away, and since then, Donald Trump's presidency has opened the way for President Xi Jinping to grab supremacy as the pinnacle Davos-endorsed "globaliser" – which within China also translates as a modern version of *tianxia*, "everything under heaven" coming within a world order orchestrated by Beijing.

The author explains that this is not a new cold war, while nevertheless constructing a narrative that contains many echoes of the first Cold War. But today China is immersed in the wider world, and especially in Western countries – including many millions of students, tourists, migrants, investors and traders – in ways that were unthinkable for the old era. And Western business has a heavy strategic involvement within China, in both manufacturing and retail – though Australian investment remains modest, with not a single significant fresh announcement since

the free trade agreement came into effect in December 2015.

The economic transformation of China has provided Xi with the platform for generating, Rachman says, "the military, diplomatic and technological resources that translate into international political power" – strong threads indeed, although he underplays the role of "soft power," which China covets, and where the West continues to dominate. Even within its own East Asian neighbourhood, China's soft power – its cultural reach from brands to lifestyle products to music, movies and soaps, respect for its academic might and analytical experts, and the influence of its ideas and its form of governance – arguably lags behind that of Japan and South Korea. And attempts to trade on traditions dating back to Confucius are undercut by the scrupulous overlooking of Chinese history by the party-state, which less than fifty years ago ordered the destruction of Confucius's symbolic "tomb," and by its recently revived insistence on Marxist education, a nineteenth-century European heritage.

The chief problem with Rachman's book is that it fails

adequately to address the core question for the world as it determines whether or how to limit China's ambitious leaps: what is the nature of the "China" that is ascending?

Externally, China appears more self-confident than ever – for instance, contemptuously brushing aside the verdict of the international court on its South China Sea annexation with impunity, and despatching People's Liberation Army forces to exercise as far away as the Baltic, and to establish their first foreign base, in Djibouti. But domestically, the party-state is focused on controlling China's real and virtual worlds in a stricter and more pervasive manner than seemed imaginable even in the country's comparatively liberal years – the 1980s up to the Tiananmen crackdown in 1989, and the late 1990s through to Xi's ascension as party chief in 2012.

This indicates a core anxiety about legitimacy, about continuity, and above all about power. After sixty-eight years of one-party rule, and with diminished debate within, is the "China model" one that is set to sweep the world? It has obvious appeal to the leaders of similarly authoritarian regimes such as Russia or Turkey, but less so to the broader world, including other nations in Asia.

But the Beijing regime remains largely opaque. Compared with the power elites of the West, those in China are unapproachable, although not entirely unknowable. Their speeches and statements are from time to time available, but are too often disregarded as "just rhetoric," or as emanations of a worldview that Westerners find outmoded, irrelevant or simply impossible to understand. The Chinese approach to political life and popularity appears strange – for instance, a lively, anecdote-laden speech would be viewed as dangerously ingratiating, akin to confessing a loss of self-confidence or, worse, of authority. China's current rhetoric on core domestic issues – rather than that on display at grand global set pieces – does not reflect a broader "Eastern" worldview.

None of China's neighbours except North Korea, for instance, could consider banning seven topics from educational discussion, as Beijing has done under a Party communiqué: constitutional democracy, civil society, economic liberalisation, media freedom, historical critiques of the Party, challenges to socialism with Chinese characteristics, and universal values. Most of these are pillars of Asian life elsewhere today.

Rachman mentions "discussing the roots of America's 'addiction' to primacy with senior US policymakers." That he doesn't apply such scrutiny to China's ambition is perhaps natural, without any such access to senior figures there.

He views South-East Asia as being "overshadowed" by China. Of course Beijing looms large. It has a great deal to offer. But a reticence remains. The American rise was also accompanied by caveats, but of a different order.

One of the differences between the United States and China, on which Rachman was unable to expand on in this tightly written book of 260 pages, is that the former appears destined to reinvigorate its demographic profile more readily, through immigration. China – like virtually all its "Easternisation" neighbours – resists immigrants. It remains all but impossible for a person who is not ethnically Chinese to become a citizen.

The West also, Rachman points out, appears set to maintain its legal and financial "institutional edge," although Belt and Road and other initiatives of the Xi era will potentially reduce the gap.

Will we ever see a multipolar world, as diplomatic experts in China itself once advocated, or are those idealistic "borderless" days now vanishing as both terrorism and economic opportunism trigger nationalist pushbacks?

Rachman's book raises, though without painting detailed scenarios, the prospect of war between the rising and falling powers. But it mentions only in passing Kim Jong-un, known ubiquitously in China as "Jin San Pang" – "Fatty Kim III." Kim is the joker in the pack most likely to trigger a war, but he hardly fits Rachman's recipe for "Easternisation." This is a reminder that books on geopolitics – and this is essentially a good one – need big themes to grab readers' attention, but risk becoming outflanked by events and people who do not fit them.

Rowan Callick

Crossing the Line: Australia's
Secret History in the Timor Sea
Kim McGrath
Black Inc.

This book will make
Australia's foreign
ministers and diplomats
squirm. They've long
been pilloried for
choosing "Kissingerian realism"
over "Wilsonian idealism" (in
Richard Woolcott's frank words)
in supporting Indonesia's case
with Timor-Leste only to see an
independent state emerge after all.
Kim McGrath has now explored a
dollar-driven dimension to their
actions – an agenda which may yet
come undone as well. She shows
how Canberra used duplicitous
diplomacy to get advantageous
maritime borders fixed in the
Timor Sea: first with Indonesia,
before word of big oil and gas

discoveries got out, then with a weak
Timor-Leste.

In both cases, Canberra took
advantage of states emerging from
collapse to push what it knew to
be a spurious geological argument
that the 3000-metre Timor Trough,
running close and parallel to
the Timor coast, was the natural
boundary of Australia's continental
shelf. Its own Bureau of Mineral
Resources, Geology and Geophysics
advised, in a February 1970 paper,
that the shelf extended beyond
Timor, the trough just a ripple in it.
Negotiators from the foreign affairs
and attorney-general's departments
suppressed this advice. Those
arguing Australia's interests were
better served by not pulling a swifty
on its neighbour – Liberal minister
David Fairbairn and diplomat Robin
Ashwin – were "laughed out of
court." Indonesia's negotiators, led
by Mochtar Kusumaatmadja, had an
inkling of the geological evidence,
which would have put the boundary
further south, along the median line
between opposing coasts. But they
were outgunned in legal resources,
the Australian Secret Intelligence
Service filched their negotiating
positions, and eventually President

Suharto overruled them to show he was no Sukarno. Later, as foreign minister, Mochtar and his successor, Ali Alatas, parlayed Australia's eagerness to open up oil and gas fields in the Timor Gap, south of the former Portuguese colony, to extract de jure recognition of its brutal occupation and a shared development zone between the Timor Trough and the median line.

McGrath sums up this sorry exercise: "The elite of Australia's bureaucracy, the most highly educated and brightest men of their generation … were so committed to Kissingerian realism that they covered up reports of massacres, torture and mass starvation in pursuit of what they believed to be Australia's national interest."

In its defence, this elite would say that at the time it seemed in Australia's interest to have Portuguese Timor inside Indonesia; the oil was just the icing on the cake for their political masters. But the Indonesian army trashed hopes of peaceful annexation: one of Jakarta's planners, Jusuf Wanandi, upon whom Australia relied, has written of his own dismay at its atrocious performance.

But even after Timor-Leste gained independence, Canberra stayed on the hook of its own fallacious, venal policy. The fragile new state reluctantly submitted to Alexander Downer's table-thumping diplomacy and continued the shared resources zone, with some favourable adjustments. They had little choice: the Howard government had withdrawn Australia from the jurisdiction of international courts on maritime boundary issues. But the revelation that ASIS spied on these negotiations too opened the way for Timor-Leste to force Canberra to argue before conciliators from The Hague in 2017. In September, the two governments announced a "breakthrough" (details are being finalised).

McGrath, the Research Director at the Steve Bracks AC Timor-Leste Governance Project, has worked with the former Victorian premier advising Timor-Leste's Xanana Gusmão since 2007. She says she is "in awe" of Gusmão's "strategic genius," but doesn't go into his endgame if he achieves the median line boundary. Bringing the large and high-quality Greater Sunrise gas field under Dili's full control might then require Indonesian cooperation; the gas field's operators, Woodside Petroleum, would still baulk at a pipeline across the trough to land the gas in Timor.

Whether Timor-Leste gets more of Greater Sunrise than the 50 per cent Downer conceded, and

gets it developed before Dili's US$16 billion petroleum fund runs out (on current draw-downs, in 2026), along with economic independence, is Gusmão's gamble. Whether some in Jakarta declare bad faith and demand renegotiation of the 1972 treaty is Canberra's gamble.

Hamish McDonald

Superfast Primetime Ultimate Nation: The Relentless Invention of Modern India
Adam Roberts
Profile Books

Narendra Modi's global ambitions were clear on his first day in office. Previous Indian prime ministers were sworn in at understated ceremonies. Modi's jamboree in 2014 was different:

"The event had a Disneyfied air of a coronation," as Adam Roberts puts it in his excellent new book, *Superfast Primetime Ultimate Nation*.

More than 4000 guests attended the glitzy New Delhi gathering, where an assortment of Bollywood stars sat alongside the leaders of India's South Asian neighbours – including Pakistan's then leader, Nawaz Sharif. Roberts, the former India correspondent for the *Economist*, describes chatting to a local politician in the crowd who predicted that "Modi will make India a hundred times stronger."

Hobbled both by socialism and its belief in "non-alignment," India had long played what Roberts describes as a "puny" role in world affairs. At its worst, this foreign policy was narrowly parochial, shunning global responsibilities and focusing on issues affecting its own borders: notably, its fraught ties with Pakistan.

Under Modi, much of this has changed. Inviting the heads of all eight nations in the South Asian Association for Regional Cooperation (SAARC) to his inauguration signalled a belated attempt to improve its traditionally bad-tempered regional relations. In mid-2015 Modi's cerebral foreign secretary, Subrahmanyam Jaishankar, announced a broader aspiration to become a "leading" rather than a "balancing" power in Asia.

But, as Roberts notes, India's geopolitical aspirations rest above all on managing its ties with both Pakistan and China. In this, Modi's record has been less promising. Peacetime relations with Islamabad have rarely been worse, spurred by acrimony over the disputed region of Kashmir. SAARC has basically broken down in the face of simmering friction between its two largest members.

Even more alarming has been the deterioration of relations with China, leading, in June 2017, to a tense military stand-off near the Bhutanese border. "Bhutan is probably the only South Asian country where India has no serious worry about Chinese influence," Roberts writes – a widely held opinion until just a few months ago, underlining the speed at which the region's security environment is changing.

India's geopolitical ambitions are generally welcomed in the West, a view Roberts shares. Its position as a counterweight to China leads many nations to seek deeper ties with New Delhi. Certainly, India has grown ever closer to the United States over the last decade. There is talk of reviving the so-called "Quad" grouping of Australia, Japan, India and the US, partly to help New Delhi play a greater maritime role in what is now often called the "Indo-Pacific."

Whether all this will be good for India remains unclear, however. Conflict with China is unlikely, but not implausible. Stronger ties with the US would do little to disguise India's weak military position relative to its more economically advanced neighbour. Here, Modi's bold style is perilous. India's ambitions are rising, but the odds of a potentially punishing miscalculation are rising with them.

James Crabtree

Refuge: Transforming a Broken Refugee System

Alexander Betts and Paul Collier

Allen Lane

REFUGEES

No one is less powerful than someone asking for help. And few politicians prioritise the needs of those who can't vote. So it should come as no surprise that for the last fifty years little political attention has been dedicated to developing a humane, sustainable and efficient way to deal with the inevitability of refugee crises.

As millions of people fled conflict in Syria in 2015 and many of those kept moving through neighbouring countries and into Europe, politicians in rich countries were forced to confront the simple reality that leaders of many developing countries have been confronting for decades: the current global framework for responding to the post-conflict movement of large numbers of refugees is failing badly.

In *Refuge: Transforming a Broken Refugee System*, political scientist Alexander Betts and economist Paul Collier expose the enormous human, political and economic costs associated with the current refugee framework and lay out a new roadmap for what an equitable and efficient approach might be.

Betts and Collier examine the flaws with the approach that was developed to deal with European refugees after World War II and is still used today to deal with the 65 million people whose lives have been uprooted by violence. The authors describe the plight of millions of people spending years, and often decades, in "temporary camps," and make a persuasive case that such camps, originally built to save lives in the short term, are destroying them in the long term.

They confront readers with the fact that the ethics of not just offering refuge but providing a new start in life are as complex as they are passionately debated. For example, is the fact that rich countries spend

$135 on the minority of refugees who cross borders to escape conflict for every $1 they spend helping those who stay behind evidence of generosity or inequity?

Refuge is at its most optimistic, and most challenging, when it urges readers to see refugees through the economist's prism of "human resources," with time, skills, creativity and entrepreneurial talent that can benefit their temporary host countries, the countries they will hopefully return to (post-conflict) and the global economy. While limitations on the ability of refugees to work and trade are often justified on economic grounds, Betts and Collier make a persuasive case that such restrictions impose devastating personal and economic costs on both refugees and host countries.

So what is to be done? The authors draw heavily on their recent experience in Jordan, where they saw firsthand efforts to combine the underutilised labour of refugees with underutilised capacity in the £100 million King Hussein bin Talal Development Area that had already been built nearby. While they are at pains to avoid "one size fits all" suggestions, a central argument is

that "special economic zones" might create win-win outcomes, especially when rich countries offer special trade concessions for goods produced within such zones.

While it is hard to argue with the proposition that refugees have an enormous amount to contribute to local and global economies, it is doubtful that most countries would be willing to invest in the kind of infrastructure that, by coincidence, lay idle near the Jordanian refugee camps. Similarly, while it is easy to see why European countries might consider granting trade concessions to products exported from a special economic zone in the midst of a crisis on their doorstep, it is harder to imagine governments in Australia, the United States or Europe offering trade concessions to similar camps in Africa or South-East Asia. Despite these difficulties, which the authors concede, the case for switching our view of refugees from burden to resource is fundamentally important, as evidenced by the breadth and stature of the endorsements on the back of the book, which range from former UN Secretary-General Kofi Annan to Nobel Prize–winning economist George Akerlof.

The premise of *Refuge*, that we need to develop structures to deal with the new realities of conflict-induced mobility, is both a strength and a weakness. It challenges readers to think about opportunities, but, understandably, does not offer a utopian solution. However, the book does map the ethical, economic and legal terrain that any designers of a new global solution will need to navigate, and provides both a challenge and a resource for all readers interested in incremental or radical change to refugee policy.

Richard Denniss

NEXT ISSUE: FEBRUARY 2018

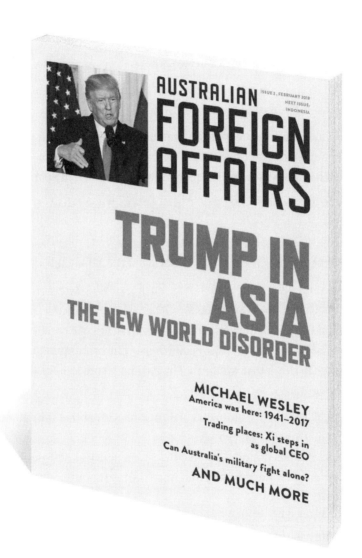

AUSTRALIAN

FOREIGN AFFAIRS

ISSUE 2, FEBRUARY 2018
NEXT ISSUE:
INDONESIA

TRUMP IN ASIA
THE NEW WORLD DISORDER

MICHAEL WESLEY
America was here: 1941–2017

Trading places: Xi steps in
as global CEO

Can Australia's military fight alone?

AND MUCH MORE

AUSTRALIAN FOREIGN AFFAIRS

The Back Page

THE THUCYDIDES TRAP

What is it: The risk of war between two great powers as one rises.

Who coined it: Graham Allison (professor, Harvard), warning of a possible conflict between China and the United States.

Where it comes from: Thucydides (historian, Athens), explaining the causes of the Peloponnesian War (431 BCE): "What made war inevitable was the growth of Athenian power and the fear which this caused in Sparta."

Who buys it: Xi Jinping (president, China): "We all need to work together to avoid the Thucydides Trap."

Malcolm Turnbull (prime minister, Australia): "If I may be accused for lapsing back into Greek history, [we must] avoid the Thucydides Trap."

Who doesn't: David A. Welch (historian, author of *Why International Relations Theorists Should Stop Reading Thucydides*): "No modern doctor would base his or her medical practice on the writings of Erasistratus, Herophilus, or Hippocrates, but for some reason International Relations scholars seem to think that whatever Thucydides wrote almost 2500 years ago still applies today."

Comments: Thucydides' arguments are ancient and subtle – which means they offer something for everybody.

Thomas Hobbes (founder, modern Western political philosophy) wrote that Thucydides hated democracy and was "the most politic historiographer that ever writ."

Irving Kristol (godfather, neoconservatism) called Thucydides' *Histories* "the favourite neoconservative text on foreign affairs," and saw it as a parable of democracy promotion.

Shelf-life: The Thucydides Trap's real trap is drawing too many lessons from an esoteric history of alien and superstitious peoples, written two millennia ago.